GOD'S CHOSEN KING

THE STORY BIBLE SERIES

1. *God's Family* tells the story of creation, God's promises to Abraham's family, and the adventures of Joseph.

2. *God Rescues His People* tells about Israel's escape from Egypt, Moses and the Ten Commandments, and the wandering in the wilderness.

3. *God Gives the Land* tells the story of Joshua, the adventures of the judges, and the story of Ruth.

4. *God's Chosen King* tells about Samuel, Saul, and David, God's promises to David's family, and the Psalms.

Additional books in the series will tell stories from the rest of the Old Testament and from the New Testament.

Story Bible Series, Book 4

GOD'S CHOSEN KING

*Stories of God and His People:
1 Samuel, 2 Samuel, 1 Chronicles, Psalms*

Retold by Eve B. MacMaster
Illustrated by James Converse

HERALD PRESS
Scottdale, Pennsylvania
Kitchener, Ontario
1983

Library of Congress Cataloging in Publication Data

MacMaster, Eve, 1942-
  God's chosen king.

  (Story Bible series; bk. 4)
  Summary: Retells the Old Testament stories of
Samuel and Saul, Saul and David, and David the King.
    1. Bible stories, English—O.T. Samuel. 2. Bible
stories, English—O.T. Chronicles, 1st. 3. Bible
stories, English—O.T. Psalms. [1. Bible stories—
O.T.] I. Converse, James, ill. II. Title.
III. Series.
BS551.2.M2959   1983   220.9'505   83-12736
ISBN 0-8361-3344-7 (Pbk.)

GOD'S CHOSEN KING
Copyright © 1983 by Herald Press, Scottdale, Pa. 15683
  Published simultaneously in Canada by Herald Press,
  Kitchener, Ont. N2G 4M5
Library of Congress Catalog Card Number: 83-12736
International Standard Book Number: 0-8361-3344-7
Printed in the United States of America
Design: Alice B. Shetler

83 84 85 86 87 88 89 10 9 8 7 6 5 4 3 2 1

The Story of This Book

Several years ago I was looking for a Bible story book to read to my children. I wanted one that was complete, without tacked-on morals or a denominational interpretation. I wanted one that was faithful to the Bible and fun to read. I couldn't find what I was looking for.

With the encouragement of my husband, Richard MacMaster, I approached Herald Press with the idea of the series: a retelling of the whole Bible with nothing added and nothing subtracted, just following the story line through the Old and New Testaments.

The people at Herald Press were agreeable and enthusiastic and gave much valuable advice, especially book editor Paul M. Schrock.

At his suggestion, I asked some academic and professional people in our community to check the stories for style and accuracy. This advisory committee, who have kindly volunteered their time, includes Bible professors George R. Brunk III, Ronald D. Guengerich, G. Irvin Lehman, and Kenneth Seitz; childhood curriculum and librarian specialists Elsie E. Lehman and A. Arlene Bumbaugh; and book marketing specialist Angie B. Williams.

I hope this series will lead its readers to the original, for no retelling is a substitute for the Bible itself. The Bible is actually a collection of books written over a long period of time in a variety of forms. It has been translated and retold in every generation, because people everywhere want to know what God is like.

The main character in every story is God. The plot of every story is God's activity among his people.

The first book in the series is called *God's Family*. It tells about beginnings: creation, human failure, and God's choice of Abraham's family to begin the work of salvation.

The second book is called *God Rescues His People*. It tells about salvation: the escape from Egypt, Moses and the Ten Commandments, and the wandering in the wilderness.

The third is called *God Gives the Land*. It tells about promises fulfilled: Joshua and the conquest, the judges, and the story of Ruth.

This book, *God's Chosen King*, is the fourth in the series. It tells about requests: Hannah's request for Samuel, the people's request for a king, the story of Saul, and the story of David. David was the model of the perfect king, but he was also a very real human being.

This volume is dedicated to the three children who inspired the series: Samuel, Thomas, and Sarah MacMaster, gifts to their parents from God.

Eve MacMaster
Bridgewater, Virginia
March 12, 1983

Contents

Stories About Samuel and Saul
1. Hannah's Prayer — 11
2. God Calls Samuel — 17
3. The Philistines Capture the Ark — 23
4. God Strikes the Philistines — 28
5. The People Ask for a King — 33
6. The Man Who Looked for Donkeys and Found a Kingdom — 38
7. Saul Becomes King — 44
8. The Broken Appointment — 48
9. Jonathan in Danger — 52
10. God Rejects Saul — 58

Stories About Saul and David
11. God Chooses David — 65
12. The Story of David and Goliath — 69
13. Saul Turns Against David — 76
14. The Secret of the Arrow — 81
15. The Massacre of Eli's Family — 86
16. David the Outlaw — 91
17. Abigail Saves David — 95
18. A Close Call — 100

19. David Escapes to the Philistines — 104
20. A Ghost Story — 109
21. Saul's Last Battle — 113

Stories About David the King

22. Two Kings Mean Trouble — 119
23. The Murder of Abner and Ishbaal — 123
24. David Becomes King of Israel — 128
25. David Brings the Ark to Jerusalem — 133
26. God Blesses David — 138
27. David's Sin — 144
28. The Beginning of David's Family Troubles — 151
29. Absalom's Rebellion — 156
30. Advice for Absalom — 162
31. News for David — 167
32. The Census, the Plague, and the Altar — 172
33. David Prepares a House for the Lord — 176
34. A Songbook for God's People — 181

Maps

1. The World of Samuel, Saul, and David — 189
2. David's Empire — 190

The Author — 191

Stories About Samuel and Saul

Hannah's Prayer

1 Samuel 1—2

HANNAH was unhappy. Her husband, Elkanah, loved her, but she had no children. Elkanah's other wife, Peninnah, teased Hannah because she had children and Hannah didn't.

Hannah and her family were Israelites, and every year they went to the city of Shiloh to worship the Lord their God. At Shiloh stood the tabernacle, a special place where the people of Israel met together for worship. The happiest times of the year were the great festivals which brought people from all over the land of Israel to

Shiloh to sing and dance and pray and offer sacrifices to the Lord.

One year Hannah did something unusual at the tabernacle.

During the fall festival each family offered an animal as a sacrifice to the Lord. Then they boiled the meat and feasted on it. Every year Elkanah divided the meat, giving Peninnah pieces for herself and each of her children. To Hannah he gave just one piece.

This year Peninnah said especially cruel things to Hannah when the meat was divided. Hannah cried and refused to eat.

"Why are you crying?" asked Elkanah. "Go on, eat! Don't be sad. Surely I mean more to you than ten children!"

But Hannah was miserable. At the end of the meal she got up from the table and went out alone to the entrance of the tabernacle. There she cried bitterly and prayed to the Lord.

The high priest, a man named Eli, watched Hannah as she prayed. From his seat beside the entrance of the tabernacle he could see her lips moving, but he couldn't hear what she was saying.

"Lord Almighty!" Hannah was praying. "Please listen to me! Please notice my misery and give me a son! If you do, I promise to dedicate him to you. My son will belong to you in a special way his whole life! Oh, please answer my prayer!"

Hannah stood there so long, mumbling to herself, that Eli began to suspect that she was drunk.

"Enough!" he finally said. "Stop this drunken behavior! Go rest until the wine wears off!"

"I'm not drunk!" said Hannah. "I haven't had any wine. I've been praying under my breath, pouring out my troubles to the Lord, because I'm so unhappy!"

"Then go in peace," said Eli, "and may the God of Israel answer your prayer."

"Thank you, sir," said Hannah. "I hope you'll always think kindly of me."

Then, no longer sad, she went back to the place where her family was feasting and she sat down and ate with them.

The next day Hannah and her family returned to their home in the town of Ramah. Soon afterward, the Lord answered Hannah's prayer.

The following autumn Hannah gave birth to a son. She named him Samuel, which means "he who is from God," "because," she said, "I asked the Lord for him."

When it was time to go to Shiloh again, Hannah told Elkanah, "I'll stay home and nurse the baby. When he's a little older, I'll take him there to stay. I'll dedicate him to the Lord, as I promised."

"Do what you think best," answered Elkanah. "Stay here until the child is older. And may the Lord help you keep your promise!"

That year Hannah's husband went to Shiloh without her. When he arrived at the tabernacle, Elkanah offered a special sacrifice to thank the Lord for their son Samuel.

A few years later Hannah took Samuel to Shiloh. She also took some gifts to offer to the Lord. After she presented her offering, she went with Elkanah and Samuel to see Eli, the high priest.

"Pardon me, sir," she said. "I'm the woman who was standing here several years ago during

the festival, praying to the Lord. I asked God for a son, and he gave me this boy. I promised to dedicate my son to the Lord, so here he is!"

Hannah left Samuel with Eli, to live in the tabernacle and serve the Lord. Before she returned home, she prayed to the Lord. Her prayer is known as "The Song of Hannah."

The Song of Hannah

The Lord has made me happy;
   He's given me success!
The Lord our God is holy;
   I sing of his greatness!

Don't take pride in your victories;
   Don't brag about your deeds!
For it's God who makes things happen;
   He balances all needs!

The Lord lets the mighty fall,
   gives weapons to the weak,
Lets the fat ones go hungry,
   and the skinny ones grow sleek!

The wife who had no children
   now has seven sons,
While the mother of a dozen
   loses every one!

For it's God who gives us life,
   and it's God who brings us death!
He can raise up the dead—
   there's power in his breath!

He makes some people low and poor,
   others high and rich,
Pulls some up out of poverty,
   throws others in the ditch!

He lifts up the humble poor
   and puts them in the seat
At the head of the great table
   where the high and mighty eat!

No person living on this earth
   has power enough alone.
It's God who wins all victories!
   Great things he has done!

2

God Calls Samuel

1 Samuel 2—3

EVERY year Hannah and Elkanah went to Shiloh to visit their son Samuel. Every year Hannah made a new robe to bring to her little boy. The robes were made of linen, just like the robes the priests wore in the tabernacle.

Every year Hannah and Elkanah went to see Eli, and every year Eli blessed them and said, "May the Lord give you more children to take the place of the one you've given to him."

Hannah had three more sons and two daughters. They stayed at home in Ramah while

Samuel grew up in the tabernacle. He dressed like a little priest, served the Lord, and helped Eli.

Eli had two sons of his own, grown men named Hophni and Phinehas. Like their father, they were priests, but they were greedy.

All the priests had certain privileges, including the right to keep part of some offerings. They were allowed to take a piece of offering meat when it was cut up and boiled. They were supposed to take whatever piece of meat happened to be pulled out of the cooking pot with a fork.

But Eli's sons didn't follow the rules. They didn't take just any piece of meat. They took the best part, even before it was cooked, and they took parts which were supposed to be burned as sacrifices to the Lord. If anyone said anything to them, Hophni and Phinehas threatened them.

When Eli heard about his sons' wicked behavior, he went to them and said, "Everyone's telling me what you do with the offerings. You know that's a great sin, for the offerings are gifts for God. Why do you do such things? If you were sinning against another person, God could help you, but you're sinning against God himself!"

Hophni and Phinehas paid no attention to their father.

Then one day a man came to Eli with a message from the Lord. "Why do you honor your sons more than the Lord?" he asked. "Why don't you punish Hophni and Phinehas? When they eat the best part of the offering meat, they're stealing from God!"

He gave Eli a warning. "The Lord is going to punish you!" he said. "He will bring death to the men of your family because your sons have disobeyed him. Your sons Hophni and Phinehas will both die on the same day. Later on, the rest of your family will be massacred. Only one man will escape. The Lord chose your family to be his priests, but because of this sin, he's going to find someone else!"

All this time, Samuel was faithfully serving God. He was growing and gaining favor with the Lord and all who knew him.

One night when he was a young man, Samuel heard a voice. It happened just before dawn, while the lamp in the tabernacle was still burning. Eli was asleep in his usual place, and Samuel was in his bed in the sanctuary. Since Eli was old and blind now, he often needed Samuel's help.

"Samuel! Samuel!" called the voice.

"Here I am!" he answered. It was the voice of the Lord, but Samuel didn't recognize it. He ran to Eli and said, "Here I am, for you called me."

"No, I didn't call," answered Eli. "Go back to bed."

Samuel went back and lay down.

"Samuel! Samuel!" called the voice again.

Samuel got up and went to Eli. "Here I am," he said. "You called me!"

"No, my son," the old man answered. "I didn't

call you. Go back to bed."

The third time the voice called, "Samuel!"

"You called me, and here I am!" he said to Eli.

Then Eli realized who was calling. "Go lie down," he said. "If you hear the voice again, say, 'Speak, for your servant is listening.'"

Samuel went back and lay down again.

"Samuel! Samuel!"

"Speak!" he answered. "Your servant is listening."

Then the voice said, "I'm going to do something soon which will tingle the ears of everyone who hears of it! I'm going to do what I warned Eli I would do. Tell him I'm soon going to punish his family because his sons have dishonored me and he didn't stop them."

Samuel lay down until morning, and then he got up and went about his work as usual. He was afraid to tell Eli what he had heard.

"Samuel, my boy!" called Eli.

"Here I am!" he answered.

"What message did the Lord give you? Tell me! May God punish you if you hide one word of his message from me!"

Samuel told Eli everything he had heard.

"He is the Lord," said Eli. "Let him do what he wants."

The news soon spread all over the land of Israel that the Lord had called Samuel. The Lord spoke to Samuel again, and every time Samuel had a message from God, the people listened. They

realized that he was a prophet, a person especially chosen to bring God's word to God's people.

Samuel was also a judge, a special leader sent by God to save the people from their enemies.

Many years earlier the Lord God had rescued the Israelites from the land of Egypt, where they were slaves. He had led them across the great and terrible wilderness to the land of Canaan. The Lord had defeated their enemies and given them everything they needed. But after living in the land a while, the people forgot the Lord. They ignored his teachings and disobeyed his commandments. Instead of living the way God wanted them to live, the Israelites copied the Canaanites who lived around them. They even worshiped the Canaanite gods.

Every time this happened, the Lord let other nations conquer his people and rule over them. Finally, the Israelites would call on the Lord for help. They would be sorry and they would ask God to forgive them. Then the Lord would send someone to help them, to save them from their enemies.

In the days of Hannah and Eli, the Israelites needed such a savior, and God sent Samuel.

3

The Philistines Capture the Ark

1 Samuel 4

AS Samuel grew up and Eli grew old, Eli's sons continued to dishonor the Lord. Many other Israelites were sinning, so the Lord let their enemies defeat them.

In those days the Philistines were Israel's most dangerous enemy. The Philistines had entered the land of Canaan about the same time as the Israelites.

The Philistines came from the islands of the Great Western Sea, bringing with them strong iron tools and weapons and a high, advanced culture. They were superior to the Israelites in almost every way.

By the time Samuel had grown up, the Philistines controlled the land along the seacoast. From time to time they came up out of their cities and raided the Israelites who lived in the hill country.

One year the Philistines sent an army up to the border of Israelite territory. The Israelites gathered together to defend themselves. The Philistines attacked the Israelite army and killed many of them.

The survivors returned to the Israelite camp, defeated and discouraged.

"Why did the Lord let the Philistines defeat us?" the leaders asked each other.

"Let's go get the ark!" one of them suggested.

"Yes!" the others agreed. "Then the Lord will save us from our enemies!"

The ark was Israel's most valuable possession. It was a wooden box covered with gold and decorated like a royal throne. God is a spirit and he is everywhere at all times. But in a special, mysterious way, he was with his people in the ark. He was their king, and the lid of the ark was the footstool of his throne. God's throne was invisible, because he himself was invisible.

The Lord wouldn't allow his people to make images of him, as other nations made idols of their gods. But he let them have the ark to remember that he was always with them.

Now the leaders of the people sent messengers to Shiloh to ask the priests to bring the ark from its resting place in the tabernacle. They wanted to take the ark with them into battle. They were sure they could make God fight for them.

A little while later Hophni and Phinehas, the sons of Eli, arrived with the ark. As soon as the soldiers saw the ark, they shouted out a great battle cry.

"What's that great roar coming from the Hebrew camp?" the Philistines asked each other. ("Hebrew" was a name that other nations called the Israelites.)

When they found out about the ark, they were terrified.

"The gods have come into their camp!" they cried.

"What can we do?"

"Nothing like this has ever happened to us!"

"We're lost!"

"Who can save us from the power of their God?"

"He's the mighty God who defeated the Egyptians!"

Finally, one of their leaders said, "Be brave, Philistines! Fight like men, or we'll all become slaves of the Hebrews!"

In the other camp, the Israelites were remembering the old stories about the ark. When God gave his people the Promised Land, the ark led them in battle. Surely, the ark would bring them victory!

But to their great surprise, the Israelites were

defeated. Many were killed, including the sons of Eli. Worst of all, the ark of the Lord was captured!

A messenger ran to Shiloh with the news, and when he told the people of the city, they cried out loud.

"What's that sound?" asked Eli. The old blind priest was sitting on top of the wall of the city gate, waiting to hear the news.

The messenger called up to him, "I've just escaped from the battle! I've run all the way here."

"How did it go, my son?" asked Eli.

"The Israelites ran away from the Philistines!

Our army was defeated and both your sons have been killed—and the ark of God has been captured!"

When he heard about the ark, Eli fell over backward from his seat. He was so old and fat, the fall broke his neck and he died.

4

God Strikes the Philistines

1 Samuel 5—6

AFTER the Philistines won the battle and captured the ark, they took it down to Ashdod, one of their five great cities. There they set the ark up inside a temple as a trophy of their victory. They left it beside the image of their god, Dagon.

Early the next morning, when the people of Ashdod went to the temple, they found the statue of Dagon lying on its face in front of the ark of the Lord. They lifted their god up and stood him back in his place.

The next day they came back and found Dagon back on his face in front of the ark. This time Dagon's head and hands were broken off and lying in the doorway of the temple.

The Philistines were frightened by this sign of the Lord's power over Dagon. They were even more frightened by what happened next.

Rats swarmed from ships docked in the Philistine ports. The rats carried fleas which were infected with bubonic plague. When the fleas bit the Philistines, they broke out with horrible sores, called plague tumors, and many of them died.

"The God of Israel is punishing us and our god!" they cried. "We must get rid of his ark!"

They sent for the rulers of the five Philistine cities. "What should we do with the ark of the God of Israel?" they asked.

"Send it to Gath," the rulers answered.

So the people of Ashdon moved the ark to the city of Gath. As soon as it arrived, the people of Gath got sick.

The people of Gath sent the ark to the city of Ekron.

"Why have you brought the ark of the God of Israel here?" complained the people of Ekron. "Do you want us all to be killed? Send it away!" they begged their rulers.

But the rulers didn't know what to do, and for seven months the Philistines moved the ark from city to city. It brought death and destruction wherever it went. By late spring the ark was back in Ekron, and the Philistines were desperate.

"What should we do about the ark of the Lord?" they asked their priests and magicians. "Tell us how to get rid of it!"

"Send it back to Israel," they answered. "But don't send it back empty. Send an offering for the God of Israel. If he accepts the offering, he'll take his hand from you, and you'll be healed of this plague."

"What should we send?" they asked.

"Send something valuable," the priests and magicians said. "Something made of gold. Make golden models of the plague rats and the plague tumors. If it's really the Lord who's striking us, these gifts will make him relax his grip on us and our gods and our land!"

The Philistines carefully followed the instructions of the priests and magicians. First they made golden models of the rats and tumors. Then they made a wooden wagon and placed the golden models in it, as an offering to the Lord. They put the ark of God in the wagon along with the offerings.

Next they took two dairy cows from their calves and hitched the cows to the wagon. They put the calves back into their stalls and waited to see what the cows would do. A cow would usually go back to its hungry calf.

As the Philistines watched, the two cows pulled the wagon straight ahead, away from their hungry calves and toward Israelite territory.

The five Philistine rulers followed the wagon as far as the border. The cows never turned aside, but, mooing softly, walked into the land of Israel.

Then the Philistines were certain that the plague was a punishment from the Lord God of Israel.

As the cows and the wagon came close to the town of Beth-shemesh, some Israelites left the fields where they were harvesting wheat and ran joyfully to meet the ark.

The cows stopped beside a great stone in a field. The people of Beth-shemesh took the wooden wagon and cut it up for firewood. Then they sacrificed the two cows on the stone altar as an offering to thank the Lord for bringing back the ark.

The Philistines watched, and when they saw that the Lord had accepted their offering, they turned around and went home.

5

The People Ask for a King

1 Samuel 7—8

THE people of Israel were a nation with a difference. Their land was pleasant, but not the best in the world. They were about the same as people everywhere. They weren't especially rich or powerful or intelligent or good. But they were different.

While every other nation in the ancient world had a human king to rule over them, Israel's king was the Lord, their God. While every other nation worshiped idols, only the Israelites worshiped the Lord, who made heaven and earth.

The Lord had chosen Israel from all the nations of the earth to be his special people. He didn't choose them because they were better than other nations. They weren't. He chose them because he wanted to, because he loved them.

When the Lord chose the Israelites, he made a special agreement with them called a covenant. According to the covenant, the Lord promised to fight for his people, to give them a land of their own, and to be their God. They promised to worship him, to follow his teachings, and obey his commandments. God's commandments were written on two stone tablets which were kept inside the ark.

The Lord kept his promises. He defeated their enemies and gave them the land. He settled them in the land according to large family groups called tribes. As long as the twelve tribes of Israel loved the Lord and worshiped him, the Lord kept them safe and gave them peace in his kingdom.

But now something was terribly wrong. The Lord had let the Philistines defeat his people. He had even allowed his ark to be captured. What was going on? Why was God punishing them?

The Lord gave a message to his prophet Samuel, and Samuel sent word to the people. "If you want the Lord to help you," he said, "you must get rid of your idols! Destroy the images of foreign gods! Worship the Lord only! Then he'll set you free from the power of your enemies!"

The people did as Samuel said. Then they met together at a place called Mizpah.

"I'll pray for you," Samuel told them, and he asked the Lord to forgive the people.

The Israelites offered sacrifices to the Lord and confessed their sins. Then Samuel prayed again. As he prayed, news came that the Philistines were marching toward Mizpah.

"Don't stop praying!" the people cried to Samuel. "Ask the Lord to save us!"

Just as the Philistines began to attack, the Lord sent a great storm. He thundered from heaven with a mighty voice. The Philistines panicked and ran away, and the Israelites ran after them. They chased them all the way to the place where the other two battles had been lost.

Samuel set up a stone in that place as a monument to remember what had happened there. He named it "Ebenezer," which means "stone of help," "because," he said, "the Lord helped us here!"

As long as Samuel was judge in Israel, the Philistines stayed in their own territory down on the plain and didn't bother the Israelites up in the hill country.

Samuel judged God's people for many years. He traveled around to the towns near Ramah, settling disputes and teaching the people the ways of the Lord. At the top of a hill above Ramah he built an altar to the Lord, where he offered sacrifices and prayed for the people. He

treated everyone fairly, and the land was at peace.

When Samuel was an old man, he appointed his sons, Joel and Abijah, to be judges with him. But instead of following their father's example, Joel and Abijah were greedy and unfair. They settled disputes in favor of the people who gave them large gifts, not in favor of those who were right.

One day the leaders of the twelve tribes said to Samuel, "You're growing old, and your sons aren't following your example. Give us a king, like other nations, to rule over us!"

A king, like other nations? But the Lord was king of Israel! As Samuel thought about the people's request, he became upset. He prayed to the Lord to find out what to do.

The Lord answered, "Listen to the voice of the people and do what they ask. It's not you they're rejecting, but me! They don't want me to be king over them. Well, let them have a king like other nations. But warn them what will happen!"

Samuel went back to the people and said, "Listen to me, and I'll tell you what your king will do to you!"

Then he told the people what would happen. Many years later the kings of Israel did all the things that Samuel said they would.

"Your king will take your property," said Samuel, "and give the best part of your crops to his officials. Then he'll take away your children. He'll draft some of your sons into his army and make others plow his fields, harvest his crops, gather his grapes, and make his weapons. He'll force your daughters to work as his cooks and bakers. After he takes your children, he'll take you to be his slaves! Finally, you'll cry out to the Lord for help, but it will be too late!"

"No!" said the people. "We want to be like other nations! We want a king to judge us and lead us in battle. We want a king to rule over us!"

When Samuel told the Lord what the people had said, the Lord answered, "Listen to them. Give the people what they want. Go find them a king!"

6

The Man Who Looked for Donkeys and Found a Kingdom

1 Samuel 9—10

A YOUNG man named Saul lived in the town of Gibeah. Saul was the most handsome man in all the land, taller than anyone else in Israel.

One day some donkeys that belonged to Saul's father, Kish, happened to wander away. Kish said to Saul, "Take one of the servants and go look for the lost donkeys."

Saul and the servant left Gibeah and walked through the hill country, searching for the donkeys. On the third day they came to the town of Ramah.

"Let's go back home," Saul said to the servant. "My father will stop worrying about the donkeys and start worrying about us."

"Wait a minute," said the servant. "I just remembered something. The prophet Samuel lives here in Ramah. They say he knows everything. Let's go into town and ask Samuel where we should look for the donkeys."

"All right," agreed Saul, "but we can't just go and ask him. We need to give him a gift. But we have nothing to give him. We've eaten all the food we brought."

"Well, look here!" said the servant. "I just found a small piece of silver! We can give this to him and he'll tell us what to do!"

"Good!" said Saul. "Let's go!"

They walked up the path toward the town of Ramah, which was built on a hill. On the way they met some girls who were coming down to draw water from the well outside town.

"Is the prophet in town?" they asked.

"Yes," one of the girls answered. "We just saw him. He's here today for a feast at the altar on the hill. The people won't eat until he comes to bless the food. If you hurry, you can still catch him."

Saul and the servant went on up to the small walled city. As they were about to enter the city gate, they happened to meet an old man coming out. He was walking toward them, on his way to the hill above the town.

Saul walked up to the man and said, "Please, sir, tell me where the prophet lives."

"I am the prophet," he answered. It was Samuel. "Come with me to the hill, for you'll eat with me today. Don't worry about those donkeys you've been looking for—they've already been found. Don't worry about such things anymore, for the riches of Israel belong to you and your family!"

"Why do you speak to me like that?" asked Saul. "I'm a humble man from the tribe of Benjamin. My tribe is the smallest tribe in Israel, and my family is the least important family in the whole tribe!"

"I'll answer your questions tomorrow," Samuel said, and he led Saul and the servant up to the hill.

They found thirty guests already seated, and Samuel put Saul in the place of honor at the head of the table.

"Bring the special piece of meat," Samuel said to the cook, "the one I told you to save."

The cook brought an enormous piece of meat—the best part—and placed it in front of Saul.

"There!" said Samuel. "That's the piece we saved for you! Eat it!"

Saul ate the meat, and after the feast was over, he went back to town with Samuel. There he found a comfortable place already prepared for him to spend the night.

Early the next morning Samuel came and

woke Saul. "Get up!" he said. "It's time for you to go home!"

They walked together through the streets of Ramah. When they came to the edge of town, Samuel said, "Tell your servant to go on ahead of us. I want to speak to you privately."

After the servant left, Samuel said, "Stay here with me and I'll tell you what God says." Then he explained to Saul that God had told him to find a king. "On the day before we met," Samuel said, "the Lord told me he was sending me a man from the tribe of Benjamin, and I should anoint this man as ruler over Israel. When I saw you walking up the hill, the Lord said to me, 'This is the man I told you about. He's the one who will rule over my people.'"

Then Samuel took a small clay jar of olive oil and poured the oil over Saul's head. "This," he said, "is the sign that the Lord has anointed you to be ruler over his people."

After the anointing Samuel said, "On your way home today the Lord will show you signs so you'll know that he has really chosen you as prince over his people. First you'll meet two men who will tell you that the donkeys have been found and that your father is worried about you. A little farther on, you'll meet three men taking offerings to the Lord. They'll give you two loaves of sacred bread.

"Finally, as you come near Gibeah, you'll meet a band of prophets. They'll be dancing and shouting with joy. In front of them will be musicians, playing clarinets and lyres and tambourines. When you hear the music, the spirit of the Lord will come over you and you'll join the prophets and dance and shout. The Lord will give you a new heart. He'll make a different person of you. The Lord will be with you when all these things happen, Saul, and he'll let you know what you should do."

On his way back home Saul met the men Samuel had told him about. Then, as he came near Gibeah, he heard music and saw the prophets dancing and shouting.

The spirit of the Lord suddenly rushed over Saul, and he joined the prophets and praised the Lord. That day the Lord gave him a new heart. People who had known Saul all his life saw him dancing and shouting, and they asked each other, "What's happened to the son of Kish?" They could tell he was a different person.

When Saul arrived home, his uncle asked, "Where have you been? Your father's been worried about you."

"I was looking for the lost donkeys," he answered. "When we couldn't find them, we went to Samuel."

"What did he tell you?"

"He told us the donkeys had been found," answered Saul. But he didn't tell his uncle or anyone else the secret of the kingdom.

7

Saul Becomes King

1 Samuel 10—12

SAMUEL had found the man who was going to be the king the people had asked for. Even his name—Saul—meant "asked for." Now it was time to present Saul to the people.

Samuel called the Israelites to meet together at Mizpah. There he told them, "I have a message for you from the Lord. You have rejected the God who rescued you from slavery in the land of Egypt, the Lord who freed you from all your enemies. Only he is your Savior, but you have asked for an earthly king. Well, I have found your king!"

Then Samuel asked the people to stand in

groups of tribes and families while he cast lots to discover God's will.

Casting lots can be done by drawing straws or rolling dice or tossing marked stones on the ground. We don't know exactly how the ancient Israelites cast lots, but they used something like a pair of stones.

Samuel cast the lots, and lot fell to the tribe of Benjamin. They stepped forward and Samuel cast lots again. This time the lot fell to the family of Kish. They came forward one by one and the lots pointed to Saul. But then Saul disappeared!

"Where is he?" Samuel asked the Lord.

"Hiding among the supplies," the Lord answered.

Samuel found Saul and brought him out where the people could see him. The young man stood head and shoulders above the crowd.

"Here he is!" announced Samuel. "The Lord is giving you the ruler you asked for!"

Everyone noticed how handsome Saul was. "Long live the king!" they shouted.

One day about a month later, as Saul was coming in from plowing the fields, he heard the sound of people crying.

"What's the matter?" he asked. "Why do they sound so sad?"

He found out that messengers had arrived in Gibeah with bad news. The messengers were from the town of Jabesh in Gilead, and they reported that the Ammonites had attacked their city. Nahash, king of the Ammonites, would make peace only on one terrible condition.

"What's the condition?" asked Saul.

The messengers answered, "Nahash will let our people live, but he'll gouge out everyone's right eye. But first we have seven days to find someone to save us. So we're going all over the land of Israel with our message. If nobody rescues us, we'll all be blinded!"

When Saul heard the awful news, he was filled with the spirit of God. He sent messages throughout the land of Israel, calling for men to follow him and rescue the people of Jabesh.

He led some men from his own tribe and volunteers from the other tribes across the Jordan River and into the hills of Gilead. They surrounded the Ammonite camp outside the city of Jabesh and attacked. They defeated the Ammonites and saved the people of Jabesh from being blinded. The people of Jabesh never forgot how Saul rescued them.

Then the Israelites gathered at Gilgal to celebrate the victory over the Ammonites and to hear Samuel's farewell message.

"I've listened to you," he told them. "I've found you a king. The Lord showed you your king with the casting of the lots, and he gave your king victory over the Ammonites. Now your king will lead you, and I'll go home. Remember, when I led you, I was honest and fair. I never took anything from you."

Everyone agreed that Samuel had been a good judge over Israel.

"The Lord your God rescued you from Egypt," he reminded them. "The Lord brought you to this land and gave you everything you needed. But you turned away from the Lord and worshiped idols. Then, when you got rid of your idols, the Lord forgave you and saved you from your enemies. But now you've rejected the Lord, your Savior. You want a king instead. Well, here's your king. You're getting what you asked for!

"I'm going home now," said Samuel. "But I'll keep on praying for you. I'll keep on teaching you the ways of the Lord. Remember the Lord your God. Worship him and obey his commands, for he has done great things for his people!"

8

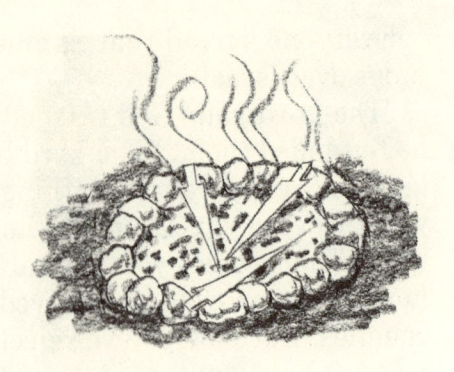

The Broken Appointment

1 Samuel 13

SOON after Saul became king, the Philistines began to bother the Israelites again. They sent raiding parties up into the hill country and they even stationed soldiers inside Israelite territory.

Saul built up his army, but the Philistines were much more powerful. They knew the secret of making iron from ore, so their weapons were stronger than the bronze ones the Israelites had.

The Israelites didn't even have any blacksmiths. When they wanted to have their plows and tools sharpened, they were forced to go to the Philistines. Only Saul and his oldest son, Jonathan, had strong weapons and shields, and none of the Israelites had horses or chariots.

One day Saul's son Jonathan killed a Philistine commander near Gibeah. This was the beginning of a war with the Philistines that lasted as long as Saul was king of Israel.

"The Hebrews have revolted!" the Philistines cried. Then they gathered an enormous army to crush the Israelites.

Saul went down to Gilgal to organize his troops. While he was there, he received a message from Samuel, telling him to wait for seven days. At the end of the seven days Samuel would come and offer a sacrifice to the Lord.

While Saul waited, the Philistine army began to march. Three units of chariots, six units of cavalry, and as many foot soldiers as there are grains of sand on the seashore entered the hill country, set up camp, and prepared for battle.

The Israelites in the hill country were so frightened that many of them ran away. Some hid among rocks and in caves, while others crossed the Jordan and escaped into Gilead.

Down at Gilgal, Saul's troops were trembling with fear. Some of them began to drift away. Finally, after seven days of waiting, Saul decided to go ahead and offer the sacrifice himself.

Just as he was finishing, Samuel arrived. "What have you done?" he asked.

"I did just what you said," answered Saul. "I waited seven days, but you didn't come! The Philistines are gathering in the hill country and my men are beginning to desert me! I thought the Philistines might march down here and attack while I was waiting. I just had to go ahead and offer the sacrifice without you!"

"You've been very foolish," said Samuel. "I gave you a command from the Lord. The Lord appointed you king, and you should have been careful of the appointment he gave you. If you had obeyed the Lord's command, he would have established you and your family as kings over Israel forever! But you broke the appointment, so your son won't become king after you. Instead, the Lord will find someone else, a man of his own choosing. He will appoint that man as prince over his people."

Then, without saying another word, Samuel left.

9

Jonathan in Danger

1 Samuel 13—14

AFTER Samuel left, Saul marched from Gilgal to the rugged hill country near Michmash. He and his six hundred men camped just a mile and a half from the Philistines. Between the armies was a deep, rocky ravine.

Soon after Saul and his forces arrived, a small Philistine outpost advanced into Michmash Pass, a narrow passage through the ravine.

That same day Saul's son Jonathan said to the soldier who carried his weapons, "Come on! Let's cross over to the camp of those heathen Philistines! Perhaps the Lord will help us. If he does, then nothing can stop us, whether we're a whole army or just two men!"

"Whatever you say," answered the servant. "I'm with you!"

They went out to the ravine without telling anyone, not even Saul.

"Let's cross over where the Philistines can see us," said Jonathan. "If they tell us to wait for them, then we'll stay on this side. But if they tell us to come up, that will be the sign that the Lord has put them into our power!"

They climbed around two great rocks and entered the ravine.

"Look!" cried one of the Philistine guards. "Some Hebrews are crawling out of their holes!"

"Come on up here!" called another guard. "We have something to show you!"

"Let's go!" Jonathan said to his servant. "The Lord's giving us the victory!"

The two men scrambled up the rocky cliff on their hands and knees. When they reached the other side, they overpowered the guards and attacked the outpost, killing twenty Philistines.

Then the Lord made the earth shake underneath the Philistine camp, throwing the whole army into a panic.

Some of Saul's watchmen told him that a mob of Philistines were running back and forth in confusion.

"Go find out what's happening!" Saul ordered.

"Are any of our men missing?"

"Jonathan and his weapon-bearer are gone!" someone reported.

Saul asked Ahijah the priest to come and ask the Lord what to do next. But then he changed his mind. "There's no time to consult the Lord," he told the priest.

Instead, Saul ordered his men to attack the Philistines. As they marched out, he told them, "Don't touch any food today! Anyone who eats before the Philistines are defeated will die! I swear to it!" And he made a solemn promise to the Lord.

Saul's army ran over to the small flat field on top of the cliff and attacked the Philistines in their camp.

They found them so confused that they were attacking each other with their swords! Even though the Israelites were outnumbered, they easily won the victory.

Then Saul's army spread out over the countryside, chasing the Philistines who escaped. But the Israelites were so weak from not eating they didn't catch many.

As Jonathan and some others ran through the fields, they found a honeycomb on the ground. It was dripping with honey. Jonathan reached out with the stick he was carrying and dipped the end of it into the honeycomb and put some honey into his mouth.

"Your father told us not to eat!" warned one of the soldiers. "While you were out of camp this morning, he ordered us to fast. He put a curse on anyone who eats today!"

"My father has been very foolish," said Jonathan. "He's hurting his own people. Our soldiers would have fought longer and better if they had eaten today! I feel much better from just a taste of this honey!"

That evening Saul said to his troops, "Let's go down tonight and catch the rest of the Philistines!"

"Whatever you think is best," answered his officers.

"Let's ask God first," suggested Ahijah the priest.

Saul asked God, "Should I attack the Philistines? Will you give us victory over them?"

But God gave no answer.

"God won't answer me!" cried Saul. "Something must be wrong! Someone has committed a sin! I promise that whoever it is will be put to death!"

No one said a word.

"Everyone stand over there," said Saul. "Jonathan and I will stand here. We'll cast lots to find out who is guilty!"

"Whatever you think is best," answered his officers.

"O Lord God of Israel!" prayed Saul. "Why haven't you answered me today? Answer me, Lord! Am I guilty of some sin? Is Jonathan? One of the soldiers? Whoever it is, let him die!"

They cast lots, and the lot fell to Saul and Jonathan.

"Cast between us!" cried Saul. "Either Jonathan or I will die!"

"No!" cried the soldiers, but Saul forced them to cast lots again.

This time the lot fell to Jonathan.

"What have you done?" asked Saul.

"I tasted some honey," he answered. "Well, go ahead. I'm not afraid to die."

"May God punish me if I don't keep my vow!" cried Saul.

"Why should Jonathan die?" asked one of the officers.

The others agreed.

"He helped win the great victory today!"

"Don't put him to death!"

"Don't let a hair of his head fall to the ground!"

"God was with him today!"

So Saul's soldiers rescued Jonathan from death.

10

God Rejects Saul

1 Samuel 15

THE victory at Michmash gave Saul some rest from the Philistines. He was able to build up his army, conquer more territory, and fight other enemies.

One day Samuel came and said, "The Lord has a message for you, Saul. Listen! He wants you to punish the Amalekites.

"Many years ago those desert raiders sneaked up on the Israelites while we were on our way out of Egypt. They attacked and killed many of us in the wilderness."

"They must be punished! Go, attack them and destroy them all!"

Saul led his army down to the southern desert. They attacked the Amalekites, chased them across the border, and defeated them in battle. But Saul didn't completely destroy them and their property. Instead, he brought back the king of the Amalekites, the best sheep and cattle, and other loot.

Then the Lord said to Samuel, "I'm sorry I made Saul king, for he has turned away from me. He doesn't obey my commands!"

Samuel felt so angry, he cried out to the Lord all night, praying for Saul. The next morning he got up early and went looking for the disobedient king. He found him at Gilgal.

When Saul saw Samuel coming, he went out to meet him. "The Lord bless you, Samuel! I have obeyed the Lord's command!"

"You have? Then what's this bleating in my ears? This mooing that I hear?"

"That's the sound of the sheep and cattle my men took from the Amalekites. They spared the best animals so we could sacrifice them here at Gilgal. I destroyed everything else, and—"

"Stop!" cried Samuel. "Not another word from you! Let me tell you what the Lord said to me last night."

"Go on, tell me."

"He raised you up and made you leader of all the tribes of Israel. He anointed you king. Now he's sent you on a mission to completely destroy the Amalekites, and you didn't obey him. Why didn't you listen to the voice of the Lord? Why did you pounce on this loot?"

"I listened to the voice of the people!" said Saul. "My men brought the animals here to sacrifice to the Lord your God."

"Do you really think the Lord wants your sacrifice when you disobey?" asked Samuel. "Obedience is better than sacrifice! You have rebelled against the Lord's command, and rebellion is as wicked as witchcraft! You have been too proud to obey God, and pride is as evil as idol worship! Because you have rejected the Lord's command, he has rejected you as king!"

"Oh, no!" cried Saul. "I have sinned! I have disobeyed the Lord and you. I was afraid of the people, and I listened to them instead of to the Lord—but please forgive me!"

"No," said Samuel. "Because you have rejected the Lord's command, the Lord has rejected you from being king over Israel!"

Then, as Samuel turned to leave, Saul caught hold of the hem of his robe, and it tore away.

Samuel said, "Even so has the Lord torn the kingdom away from you today! He has given it to another, a better man than you!"

"I have sinned," said Saul, "but please show me respect in front of my officers. Come with me while I worship the Lord your God."

Samuel went with Saul to the altar and Saul bowed down and worshiped the Lord.

Then Samuel ordered, "Bring Agag, king of the Amalekites, to me!"

The soldiers brought out their prisoner, and Samuel executed Agag right there in front of the altar.

Then Saul went home to Gibeah and Samuel returned to Ramah. They never met again while Samuel was alive, but Samuel mourned for the rejected king.

Stories About Saul and David

11

God Chooses David

1 Samuel 16

SAUL was still king, but God was going to replace him with someone else, a better man, a man of God's own choosing. Samuel was feeling sad about this, for he still loved the tall, handsome king.

One day the Lord said to Samuel, "How long will you keep on mourning for Saul? I have rejected him as king over Israel! Now I want you to go to Bethlehem in Judah, to a man named Jesse. Take a flask made of horn and fill it with olive oil, for I have found my king! You will anoint one of Jesse's sons to rule over Israel."

"How can I do that?" asked Samuel. "When Saul hears about it, he'll kill me!"

"Take a calf," said the Lord. "When you arrive in Bethlehem, tell everyone that you're there to offer the calf as a sacrifice. Invite Jesse to come to the sacrificial feast. I'll let you know what to do then."

Samuel did as the Lord commanded. He traveled across the hills from Ramah to Bethlehem, leading the young cow behind him. In his hand he carried the horn of oil.

The leaders of Bethlehem came out to meet Samuel.

"I'm here to offer a sacrifice to the Lord," he explained to them. "Come celebrate with me today."

He found Jesse and invited him to bring his family to the feast. When it was time, Jesse arrived with seven young men. Samuel looked at them carefully. Eliab, the oldest, was tall and extremely handsome.

"Surely this is the Lord's anointed king!" Samuel said to himself.

But the Lord told Samuel, "Don't pay any attention to his looks. Eliab isn't the one I have chosen. I don't look at people the way human beings do. You look into the face, but God looks into the heart."

Next Jesse presented his second son, Abinadab. The Lord rejected him.

Then he brought his third son, Shammah. He was rejected, too.

Jesse brought seven sons to Samuel, but the Lord chose none of them.

"Are these all the boys you have?" Samuel asked.

"Well, there's one more," answered Jesse. "The youngest. But he's out in the pasture taking care of the sheep."

"Send for him," said Samuel. "We won't offer the sacrifice until he comes."

When Jesse's youngest son arrived, Samuel noticed that the boy was attractive, with red cheeks and bright eyes. His name was David.

"This is the one!" the Lord told Samuel. "Anoint him!"

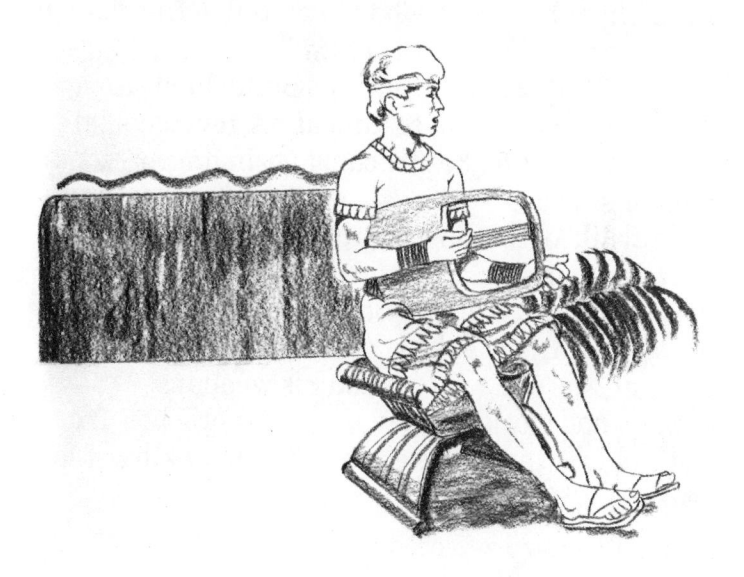

Samuel poured the oil on David's head. Immediately, the spirit of the Lord came over David. From that day on, God was with him.

Samuel told no one in David's family what the anointing meant. After the feast he returned to Ramah and David went back to the sheep.

At about the same time that the spirit of the Lord came to David, he left Saul. Saul became so depressed that everyone around him was worried.

"Let us help you," said one of his servants. "Just give the order, and we'll send for someone to play the lyre. Music will make you feel better."

"All right," said Saul. "Go find someone who plays well and bring him here."

Another servant said, "I've heard that Jesse of Bethlehem has a son who plays well, a fine young man, and the Lord is with him."

Saul sent messengers to Bethlehem to ask Jesse to send his son to Gibeah. A few days later David arrived at Saul's court, bringing presents from his father.

Saul liked the boy right away. David was an excellent musician, and when he sang and played, Saul felt much better. He was so pleased with David, he asked him to be his personal servant, the one who carried his weapons.

Saul had no idea that the shepherd boy from Bethlehem was anointed to be the next king of Israel.

12

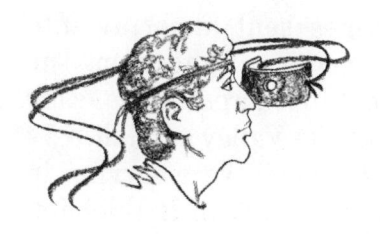

The Story of David and Goliath

1 Samuel 17—18

THE people had asked for Saul, but they loved David. Even his name—David—meant "beloved."

When David first came to Saul's court, he won Saul's love with his music. Then he won the love of Saul's oldest son, Jonathan. Jonathan gave David his royal robe, his sword, and his bow, and the two young men promised to be friends forever.

The people of Israel began to love David when he helped win a victory against the Philistines.

One year the Philistines sent an army into Judah, and Saul sent his army to fight them. The two armies camped on hills across from each other, on opposite sides of the Valley of Elah.

David's three oldest brothers were serving in Saul's army, and David was back in Bethlehem, taking care of the sheep. One day Jesse sent David to visit his brothers, to take presents to them and their officers, and to find out how they were.

As soon as David arrived at the Israelite camp,

he heard how all the soldiers were terrified of a Philistine named Goliath.

"He's a huge man—a giant!" said one of the soldiers. "He comes out of the Philistine camp every day to challenge us to single combat!"

Just then David saw someone walking across the valley toward them.

"Here he comes!" said another soldier. "He's been coming out every morning and every evening for forty days!"

David saw a huge Philistine foot soldier, almost seven feet tall. He was covered with armor. He wore a bronze helmet on his head and heavy plate armor on his body and legs. He carried a heavy bronze sword and an enormous thick spear with an iron point. Only his face was uncovered. How could any swordsman possibly wound Goliath?

"Hey, Hebrews!" the giant shouted across the valley. "What are you doing here, all lined up for battle? I'm the Philistine champion, you slaves of Saul! I dare you to send someone to fight me! Come on, choose someone! If he can beat me in a fair fight, we'll be your subjects. But if I kill your challenger, you'll have to serve us! I defy your army! I dare you to fight!"

When no one came out to fight, Goliath turned around and went back to his own camp. Saul and the whole Israelite army were too frightened to answer the challenge.

One of the soldiers turned to David and said,

"The king has promised to give a rich reward to the man who strikes down that Philistine!"

"What reward is that?" asked David. "What will the king give to the one who kills Goliath?"

"The king will give his own daughter to be the hero's wife!"

Just then Eliab, David's oldest brother, came up. He had overheard David talking with the soldiers.

"What are you doing here?" he asked. "Who's taking care of the sheep while you're gone? You rascal, you just came here to watch the fighting!"

"Now what did I do?" asked David. "I was just asking a question!"

He went to another part of the camp and talked to more soldiers. They all told him the same thing about Goliath. Someone overheard David and reported him to Saul. The king sent for him.

"My lord," said David to Saul, "don't be afraid of this Philistine! I'll fight him!"

"You can't do that!" answered Saul. "You're just a boy, and he's a professional soldier!"

"My lord," said David, "when I look after my father's sheep, I watch out for lions and bears. If one comes and carries off a lamb, I chase after it. I strike it down and snatch the lamb from its jaws! If a lion or bear attacks me, I seize it and knock it down and batter it to death. I've killed lions and bears, and I'll strike down this heathen! He has defied the army of the living God! The

Lord has protected me from the paws of wild animals, and he'll protect me from the hand of this Philistine!"

"All right," said Saul. "You may go. And may the Lord be with you!"

Then he took off his armor and gave it to David. He placed his bronze helmet on David's head and fastened his strong sword onto David's belt.

David tried to take a few steps in Saul's armor. "I can't even walk in this!" he said. "I'm not used to it!"

He took off the armor and picked up his shepherd's rod. He went out to the little stream in the valley and selected five smooth stones from the creekbed and hid the stones in his shepherd's pouch. Then he took the pouch, the rod, and his slingshot, and went out to meet Goliath.

The giant was walking toward the Israelite camp with a soldier going in front of him, carrying his shield. When Goliath saw David coming out to meet him with a shepherd's rod, he was annoyed.

"Why are you coming after me with a stick?" he cried. "Am I a dog?" Then he cursed David in the name of his god. "Come on!" he challenged. "I'll kill you and give your body to the birds of the sky and the wild beasts of the field!"

"You come against me with sword and spear," said David, "but I come against you with the name of the Lord Almighty, the God of Israel! Today the Lord will put you into my power, and I'll strike you down and cut off your head! I'll leave your body for the birds of the sky and the beasts of the field! The whole world will know that there is a God in Israel! And everyone here will know that the Lord doesn't need swords and spears to save his people!"

Goliath moved forward, expecting David to hit him with the rod.

David slowly put his hand into his pouch and took out one of the smooth stones. He placed the stone in his slingshot and slung it at Goliath. The stone struck the giant on the forehead, and he fell face down to the ground.

David ran and stood beside him. He took Goliath's sword out of its sheath and cut off the giant's head.

As soon as the Philistines realized that their champion was dead, they turned around and ran away. The Israelites chased after them, shouting the war cry. They chased them all the way to the gates of the Philistine cities!

Saul was so pleased with David, he wanted to keep him at court. "Promise to be my loyal officer," he said, "and I'll give you my daughter Merob as your wife."

"My lord," answered David, "who am I, and who are my family, to receive such an honor? I'm not great enough to marry your daughter and become your son-in-law!"

Saul gave Merob to someone else, but he made David an officer in his army. David was successful in leading troops in battle and in everything Saul sent him to do. Everyone in Israel was pleased with David.

13

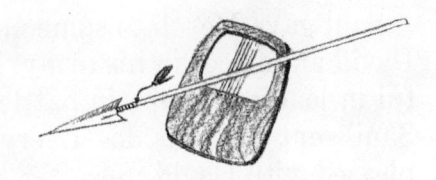

Saul Turns Against David

1 Samuel 18—19

FOR several years David served as an officer in Saul's army, and Saul was pleased with him. Then one day as David and his troops were returning from a battle, some women came out to meet them. They were dancing and playing tambourines and lutes.

"Saul has slain his thousands!" they sang, "but David has slain his ten thousands!"

When he heard about it, Saul was very angry. "They're giving David more credit than me!" he said to himself. And from that day on, he kept his eye on David. He promoted the young officer to a higher rank and put him in charge of more men and sent him out on more dangerous missions.

But David was successful in battle and in everything he did, for the Lord was with him. He won the loyalty of all the people. He was so popular that Saul was afraid to hurt him.

Then Saul's younger daughter, Michal, fell in love with David.

"Here's my chance!" thought Saul. "I'll use Michal as bait to lure David to his death!"

He sent his officials to speak to David privately. "The king is pleased with you," they said. "All his officials support you. He's willing for you to marry his daughter and become his son-in-law."

"That is a great honor," answered David, "and a high position. I can't become the king's son-in-law. I'm too poor!"

Saul's officials reported to him, and he said, "Tell David I don't expect an expensive marriage present. He can just give me a hundred dead Philistines!"

He was thinking to himself, "I mustn't kill David myself, but I'll make sure he falls into the hands of the enemy!"

When Saul's officials went back to David, David saw the chance to do what he wanted. He took his men and went out and killed a hundred Philistines. Then he came back to Saul and married his daughter.

Now Saul was really afraid of David. He realized that the Lord was with David and all the people loved him. He made up his mind to get rid of him.

One day while David was out, Saul told his officials that he had decided to kill David. Saul's son Jonathan immediately went to warn David.

"My father's looking for a chance to kill you!" he warned. "Be on your guard! Go hide somewhere until I find out what's going on."

Then Jonathan went back to his father and said, "My lord! Don't hurt David! He hasn't done anything to you. He's been your loyal friend and supporter. When he risked his life to kill Goliath, you were just as pleased as the rest of us. So why do you want to kill him?"

Saul listened carefully to Jonathan. "I won't kill David," he promised. "I swear I won't!"

Jonathan reported Saul's promise to David, and David returned to court and served Saul again.

Soon afterward, another war with the Philistines broke out, and David led his troops into battle. He won a great victory, and all Israel was pleased with him.

Then God sent an evil spirit which rushed over Saul as he was sitting in his house. He was holding his spear and listening to David play the lyre.

Saul was thinking about the song the women sang and how popular David was with everyone. Suddenly he hurled his spear at David, trying to pin him to the wall. David dodged, and the spear stuck in the wall. He jumped up and ran away from Saul's house.

That night Saul sent some men to watch David's house and kill him when he came out in the morning.

"Hurry!" said David's wife, Michal. "Get away from here tonight! If you don't, you'll be a dead man tomorrow!"

She let David down through a window, and he slipped away in the darkness. Then Michal took a large household idol and put it into David's bed.

She laid a goathair rug over its head and covered it with a blanket. It looked like a man was asleep in the bed.

The next morning, when Saul's men came to arrest David, Michal told them he was ill.

Saul's men reported to him, and he said, "I want David brought here if you have to drag him out of his bed! I want him put to death!"

Saul's men returned to David's house, and this time they went into his bedroom. They found the rug and blanket in his bed. David had escaped.

14

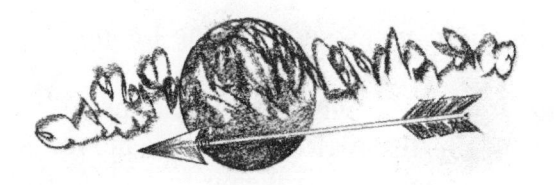

The Secret of the Arrow

1 Samuel 19—21

"WHAT have I done?" David asked Jonathan. "Why is your father trying to kill me?" After escaping from Saul, David had gone to Ramah, but Saul and his men had chased after him, so David doubled back to Gibeah and met Jonathan secretly.

"I don't believe he's trying to kill you," said Jonathan. "He promised me he wouldn't. He tells me every little thing that happens. Surely, I'd be the first to know if he'd changed his mind!"

"I don't think so," said David. "He knows how

much you care about me, so he's hiding his plans from you."

"Well," said Jonathan, "what can I do to help?"

"Tomorrow is the festival of the New Moon," said David. "Here's what I want you to do." And he told Jonathan his plan.

Jonathan agreed to David's plan. Then he said, "I have an idea. When I find out what my father's going to do, I'll send you a secret signal. I'll come out to your hiding place and shoot an arrow. I'll bring a servant to find it. If you hear me telling him that the arrow's on the near side of the target, you'll know it's safe to come back. I'm sure it will be."

Jonathan continued, "If you're right and I'm wrong—if my father really wants to kill you—then I'll give a different signal. I'll tell the servant that the arrow's on the far side of the target. That will mean that you must stay in hiding."

David agreed to Jonathan's idea. Then the two friends made a covenant and agreed to be friends forever.

"May the Lord be with you as he used to be with my father!" said Jonathan. "And may you be loyal and kind to me all my life. After I die, show loving kindness to my family, for my sake."

Then David went out to the countryside to hide, and Jonathan waited to discover what his father was planning to do.

The festival of the New Moon was a time for

resting and feasting. All the members of Saul's family and all his officers were supposed to eat with the king.

Saul came to the banquet and sat down at his usual place against the wall. His cousin Abner, commander-in-chief of Saul's army, sat next to him. Jonathan sat across the table from his father. David's place was empty.

The first day of the feast Saul said nothing about David's absence. "He's probably been delayed," he thought.

But on the second day he became suspicious. "Why is David's place empty?" he asked Jonathan.

Jonathan followed David's plan and answered, "David's in Bethlehem. He asked my permission to spend the holiday with his family."

"Traitor!" screamed Saul. "You're a disgrace to your family! Don't you understand? As long David lives, there's danger that he—and not you—will become the next king. He must die!"

"Why should David die?" asked Jonathan. "What has he done?"

Saul was so angry, he raised his spear at his son. Jonathan leaped from his seat and stormed away without eating.

The next day was the third and final day of the festival. Instead of feasting with his father, Jonathan took his bow and a quiver of arrows and went out to the countryside.

"Run!" he said to the servant boy with him.

83

"Find the arrow when I shoot!"

As the little boy ran toward the target, Jonathan shot an arrow over his head.

"The arrow is on the far side!" Jonathan shouted. "Hurry! Go get it!"

The boy found the arrow, picked it up, and brought it back to Jonathan. He didn't know it was a secret signal.

Jonathan gave the bow and arrows to the boy and sent him back to town. As soon as he was out of sight, David came out from behind a pile of rocks. He bowed down in front of Jonathan, and then they kissed each other and cried.

"Go in peace!" said Jonathan. "And always remember our covenant!"

Jonathan went home, and David wandered away, never to return to the service of King Saul.

15

The Massacre of Eli's Family

1 Samuel 21—22

DAVID'S first stop in his wanderings was the city of Nob.

Years earlier, when the Philistines had captured the ark, the priests of Shiloh had fled to Nob, taking the tabernacle with them. A great grandson of Eli now served as high priest in the tabernacle. His name was Ahimelech, and he came out to meet David.

"Why are you here all alone?" Ahimelech asked.

"I'm under orders from the king," David

answered. "He told me not to let anyone know my business. My men are waiting for me in a secret place." Then he asked, "Can you give me something to eat? Do you have any bread?"

"I have no ordinary bread," answered Ahimelech. "Only the sacred bread which is inside the tabernacle. The priests are taking it out today and putting in fresh. You may have five loaves."

"Do you have any weapons?" David asked. "A spear or a sword? I left in such a hurry, I didn't bring mine with me."

"The sword of Goliath the Philistine is here. It's wrapped in a cloth inside the tabernacle. If you want it, take it. It's the only weapon we have."

"There's no better sword anywhere!" said David. "Give it to me!"

Ahimelech gave him the bread and the sword, and David slipped away—but not before one of Saul's men saw him.

Next David went to the wilderness of Judah. He found a safe hiding place in a fortress on a hilltop in the city of Adullam. He made his headquarters there.

David's seven brothers and other relatives came out to join him, and so did many fighting men from the tribe of Judah. People with debts and other troubles came to stay with David, and soon he had an army of four hundred men.

Meanwhile, Saul was trying to find out where

David was. He sat under a tamarisk tree on a hilltop in Gibeah, his spear in his hand, and all his officers stood around him.

"Listen to me, you men of Benjamin!" he said to them. "I know you're all plotting against me! But you won't gain anything from it! You won't be the ones David rewards with fields and vineyards! You won't become officers in his army!"

He looked around at them. "You should have told me what was going on! No one told me when Jonathan helped David escape! You didn't care enough about me to tell me that my own son was working with David! You traitors! You're all working for that outlaw!"

Just then the chief of Saul's palace guard stepped forward. He was an alien, a man from Edom named Doeg.

"I've seen David," he said. "At Nob, a few days ago. I happened to be in the city when he arrived, alone and unarmed. Ahimelech, the high priest, prayed for him and gave him food and weapons."

Saul immediately sent for Ahimelech and all the other priests. His soldiers brought them from Nob to Gibeah.

"Now listen to me, Ahimelech!" cried Saul when the high priest arrived.

"Yes, my lord," he answered.

"Why have you been plotting against me? Why did you give food and weapons to David? Why did you pray for that outlaw? You helped him rebel against me!"

"My lord," answered Ahimelech, "David is your most loyal officer! He's your own son-in-law, the commander of your bodyguard! Everyone honors and respects him! Yes, I prayed for David. It wasn't the first time, either. What's wrong with that? Don't accuse me and my family of plotting against you, my lord! I know nothing about such things!"

"Ahimelech!" screamed Saul. "You and your whole family must die!"

The king turned to his soldiers and said, "Go—kill these priests, for they helped my enemy! They knew where he was and they didn't tell me!"

But Saul's men refused to lift their hands against the priests of the Lord.

"You!" cried Saul, pointing to Doeg. "You strike down these traitors!"

"Yes, my lord!" answered Doeg, and he killed all the priests who were there. Then Saul sent to Nob and he executed everyone who was in the city. Only one man escaped alive.

Abiathar, the son of Ahimelech and great-great grandson of Eli, went out to Adullam and told David about the massacre.

"I saw Doeg at Nob!" said David. "I should have known this would happen! I'm responsible. Stay here with me. The man who wants to kill me will be after you too, but don't be afraid. You'll be under my protection."

Abiathar stayed with David for the rest of his life, praying and consulting the Lord for him. After the massacre, no priest ever helped Saul again.

16

David the Outlaw

1 Samuel 23

DAVID was an outlaw, wandering from place to place, hiding from Saul. One day while he was at Adullam, he heard that the Philistines had been raiding the town of Keilah. They were stealing wheat from the threshing floors and terrorizing the people.

With the help of Abiathar the priest, David consulted the Lord. "Should I go attack those Philistines?" he asked.

"Yes," answered the Lord. "Attack them and set the city free!"

But David's men complained, "It's dangerous enough here in Adullam! It will be even worse in Keilah. Those Philistines will murder us!"

David consulted the Lord again.

"Go down to Keilah," answered the Lord, "and I'll put the Philistines into your power!"

By this time David had six hundred men. He led them down to Keilah, and they attacked and defeated the Philistines and saved the city.

Saul heard that David was in Keilah. "God has put David into my power!" he said to himself. "When he entered that walled city, he walked into a trap!"

He gathered his whole army and marched toward Keilah to lay seige to the city.

When David heard that Saul was coming, he asked Abiathar to help him again.

"O Lord God of Israel," David prayed, "I've heard that Saul is on his way here to destroy the city because of me! Is he really coming? O Lord, please answer me!"

"He's coming!" answered the Lord.

"If we stay here, will the leaders of the city hand us over to Saul?" David asked.

"They will," answered the Lord.

David left Keilah immediately. When Saul learned that David had escaped, he gave up and went back to Gibeah.

David led his men from Adullam to the wilderness of Ziph, a dry, rocky part of the wilderness of southern Judah.

One day Jonathan came out to see him. "Don't be afraid," he said, "for my father will never lay a hand on you! You'll rule over Israel, and I'll be your second-in-command! Even my father knows that!"

David and Jonathan promised one last time to be friends forever, and then Jonathan went back to Gibeah. David and his men went farther south, toward the town of Ziph.

Some people from Ziph went to Saul and said, "David is sneaking from one hiding place to another in the hills near our city. Come on down whenever you want to, and we'll help you catch him!"

"May the Lord bless you!" said Saul. "You've

saved me a lot of trouble! But you'd better go back and find out exactly where his hiding places are. David's tricky. When you find out, report to me, and I'll go with you. I'll track down that rebel if I have to look under every rock in Judah!"

The Ziphites came back a few days later and Saul took some soldiers and went out with them to the wilderness.

When David heard that Saul was coming, he took his men to the wilderness of Maon and hid behind a rocky hill. The Ziphites knew all of David's hiding places and they soon found out where he was. They led Saul to the hill. Saul split his forces into two groups. They circled around the hill, closing in on David and his men. David was trapped.

Just as Saul was about to capture David, a messenger arrived. "Come quickly!" he shouted. "The Philistines are attacking Israel!"

Saul returned to Gibeah at once. David was saved.

17

Abigail Saves David

1 Samuel 25

IN the wilderness of Maon lived a rich man named Nabal. Nabal owned a thousand goats and three thousand sheep. His wife, Abigail, was intelligent and beautiful, but Nabal was rough and bad-tempered.

One day David heard that Nabal was shearing his sheep, so he sent ten of his men with a message.

"David sends his greetings!" they told Nabal. "He has heard that you're working and celebrating out here, and he wants you to know that he has been protecting your shepherds in the wilderness. Ask them. They'll tell you. So now David wants you to give him something to pay for his kindness to your shepherds."

"Who is David?" asked Nabal. "I've never heard of him! These days the land is full of runaways setting themselves up as chiefs! Why should I give my bread and wine and meat to someone I've never heard of?"

David's men went back and reported what Nabal had said.

"Come on!" David ordered. "Put on your swords and follow me! It was a waste of time to protect that man's property out there in the wilderness! I saw to it that nothing was stolen, but he has refused to pay me. I'll kill him and all his men before the sun rises tomorrow!"

Nabal's wife, Abigail, heard that David was coming. "David's men were very good to us," one of her servants said. "They never bothered us. They really helped us. They were like a wall, protecting us while we were tending our sheep in the wilderness. But when David sent messengers to Nabal, he screamed at them! Now something terrible might happen! Our master is so mean, he won't listen to anyone!"

Abigail acted quickly. She took two hundred loaves of bread, two skins of wine, five sheep, a bushel of roasted grain, two quarts of raisins, and two hundred fig cakes and loaded them onto the backs of some donkeys.

"Go ahead with these gifts," she told her servants. Then she left home without telling her husband.

As she was riding along behind her servants, Abigail came to a pass in the hills. There she suddenly met David and his men, coming right toward her.

She quickly got down from her donkey and threw herself onto the ground in front of David. "Please, sir, listen to me!" she said. "Don't pay any attention to that rascal Nabal! Nis name means 'foolish,' and that's what he is! Please accept these gifts from me. I'm sorry I wasn't home when your men arrived."

She continued, "The Lord will bless you and your family, and no harm will come to you as long as you live. The Lord will make you ruler over Israel! That's why it's important that you don't give in to anger now! Don't take matters into your own hands. Let the Lord take revenge on your enemies. And when the Lord blesses you, remember me!"

"Praise the Lord!" said David. "He sent you to me! Thank God for your good sense! You've kept me from committing murder today! I was so angry, I was ready to take matters into my own hands!"

He accepted Abigail's gifts and said, "Go home in peace. I'll do as you have asked."

Abigail returned to Nabal, who was feasting and drinking with his friends. She saw that he was drunk, so she said nothing to him.

The next morning, when the wine had worn off, Abigail told Nabal what she had done. He was so angry, he had a stroke. He lay like a stone, completely paralyzed. Ten days later the Lord struck him again, and he died.

"Praise the Lord!" said David when he heard the news. "God has kept me from sin, and he has taken revenge on my enemy!"

Then David sent a message to Abigail, asking her to become his wife.

"I'm David's servant," she answered. "I'm ready to wash the feet of his servants. May all his enemies be like Nabal!"

Then she quickly got on her donkey, took five of her maids, and went to meet David.

In those days men often had more than one wife. Rich men and kings married many women. David had lost Michal, for Saul gave her to someone else after David left Gibeah. In Judah David had married a woman named Ahinoam, and later on he had many wives. But Abigail, David's third wife, was the most intelligent. She was the woman who saved David from himself.

18

A Close Call

1 Samuel 26

ONE day the people of Ziph went to Saul and told him that David was hiding on a hill overlooking the wilderness of Judah. Saul took his army and his commander, Abner, and went out to capture David.

When David found out that Saul was coming, he sent spies to find out where he was camped. Then he took his nephew Abishai and went out to Saul's camp at night.

The Lord sent a deep sleep over Saul and Abner and all their men, so David and Abishai were able to sneak past the soldiers. They found Saul lying in his tent in the middle of the camp, with his spear stuck into the ground next to his head.

"Here's your chance!" said Abishai. "God has put your enemy into your power! Let me plunge his spear through him! I'll pin him to the ground with one strike!"

"No!" said David. "Don't touch him, for he's the Lord's anointed king! The Lord himself will decide when it's time for Saul to die. Let's take his canteen and his spear and get out of here!"

They took Saul's spear and the small round water jar from their places by his head. No one saw them as they sneaked back out of the camp. They moved swiftly among the tents of Saul's sleeping soldiers and crossed over to the opposite side of the valley. They climbed to the top of a high hill and stood there, a safe distance from Saul's camp.

"Abner!" called David across the valley. "Abner! Can you hear me? Answer me, Abner! Answer me!"

"Who's calling?" asked Abner.

"Abner!" called David again. "You're a great man in Israel! Why weren't you doing your job tonight, Abner? Why weren't you watching over your master, the king? Someone just entered your camp to harm him! You're in trouble, Abner! You're supposed to protect the Lord's anointed, but you've failed in your duty! Where's the king's spear, Abner? Where's the water jar that was right by his head?"

Saul woke up. "Is that your voice David, my son?" he called.

"Yes, it is I," called David from the hilltop. "Tell me, my lord, why are you still hunting me? What have I done? What crime have I committed? You're like the hunters who chase the calling bird that lives in these hills!"

"Come back, David!" cried Saul. "I'll never hurt you, for you have spared my life tonight! I've been foolish! I've made a great mistake!"

"Here's your spear, my lord," called David. "Send one of your men to fetch it. See for yourself that when the Lord put you into my power, I refused to raise my hand against his anointed king."

"God bless you, my son!" said Saul.

David didn't trust Saul, so he went back to his hiding place. Saul returned to Gibeah, and the two men never met again.

19

David Escapes to the Philistines

1 Samuel 27—29; 1 Chronicles 11

"IT'S too dangerous to stay out here in the wilderness," said David to himself. "One of these days Saul will catch me and kill me. I'm going to leave Judah and go down to the land of the Philistines. There I'll be safely out of Saul's reach."

He took his six hundred men and crossed the border to the Philistine city of Gath. Achish, king of Gath, welcomed the great warrior from Judah to his territory, and Saul gave up trying to capture him.

One day David said to Achish, "Let me have a

place in one of the towns in the countryside. There's no need for my men and their families to live here in the royal city with you."

Achish agreed to give David land in the town of Ziklag, near the border of Judah. There David and his men and their families settled.

While he was living in Ziklag, David gained support from every tribe in Israel. Many experienced soldiers joined him, even some from Saul's own tribe of Benjamin. The men around David were the best and the bravest, famous warriors who were as fierce as lions and as swift as wild deer.

David took his men out on raiding parties to attack the desert tribes as far south as the Egyptian border. They brought loot back to Ziklag—sheep, cattle, donkeys, camels, and clothing. David gave some of the loot as gifts to the leaders of Judah.

When Achish questioned him about the raids, David said he was attacking Judah. All the time he was with Achish, David pretended to attack Judah while he was actually protecting Judah from the desert tribes.

Achish was so sure that the people of Judah hated David, he thought David would be with him the rest of his life. He trusted David and believed that he was loyal to the Philistines.

Sixteen months after David arrived in Philistine territory, the Philistines gathered an army to attack Israel. Achish went to David and said, "Of course you understand that you and your men must march out to battle with me against Israel!"

"Certainly!" answered David. "Now you'll see for yourself how we can fight!"

"Good!" said Achish. "I'll appoint you as my personal bodyguard!"

David and his men marched up to the hill country behind Achish's soldiers. When the Philistine commanders saw them, they were alarmed.

"What are those Hebrews doing here?" one of them asked.

"That's David," Achish answered. "He used to be one of Saul's officers, but he deserted more than a year ago and came to me. I've never had any problem with him."

But the Philistine commanders weren't satisfied. "Send David back to Ziklag!" said one. "Don't let him come into battle with us."

Then another commander asked, "Isn't he the same one the women sing about? You know— 'Saul has slain his thousands, but David has slain his ten thousands!'"

"He might betray us during the battle just to win favor with his king!" added another.

So Achish went to David and said, "I know you've been honest and loyal, and I'm pleased with your service. I'd like you to go with us. But these commanders don't trust you. You'll have to go back to Ziklag right away."

"What have I done wrong?" asked David. "If you're pleased with me, why can't I go and fight the enemies of my master and king?"

"You can't go," said Achish. "The commanders insist. Tomorrow morning, as soon as it's light enough to see, take your men and go home!"

Early the next morning David and his men returned to Ziklag, and the Philistines marched to Jezreel without him.

# 20

A Ghost Story

1 Samuel 28

WHEN Saul heard that the Philistines were coming, he led his troops to the Valley of Jezreel. They camped at the foot of Mount Gilboa.

The Philistines arrived and set up camp across the valley at the foot of the Hill of Moreh.

As Saul looked at the size of the Philistine army, his heart pounded with fear. Who could help him? Samuel? Samuel was dead. David? David was with the Philistines. The priests? They were all dead. And worse, every time that Saul asked the Lord for help, the Lord refused to answer.

In those days it was common practice to try to tell the future by reading omens or talking to ghosts, the spirits of the dead. People who call up ghosts are known as mediums. The Lord had commanded his people not to do these things, and Saul himself had banished all the fortune-tellers and mediums from the land of Israel. But now Saul was desperate. He didn't know where else to turn for help.

"Go find a medium for me," he said to his servants. "I want to consult someone who can call up the spirits of the dead."

"There's such a woman living near here, at Endor," someone said.

Saul made plans to visit Endor that evening. He didn't eat anything else the rest of the day, and after dark he took off his royal robe and put on a disguise. Then he took two men and went out. They circled around the Philistine camp to reach Endor, at the other side of the Hill of Moreh.

When he arrived at the medium's house, Saul said to the woman, "Tell my fortune! Call up a ghost. Bring up the spirit of the person I name."

"No, sir," she answered. "Haven't you heard? The king has banished all the fortune-tellers and mediums. It's against the law to consult the spirits of the dead."

She looked at the stranger. "Are you setting a

trap for me? I'll be killed if anyone finds out."

"It's all right," he answered. "As the Lord lives, I promise you won't be punished!"

"You've tricked me!" she screamed. "You're Saul!"

"Don't be afraid."

"Well, then whom shall I call up for you from the underworld?"

"Call up Samuel."

She closed her eyes and went into a trance.

"Tell me what you see!" he demanded.

"I see a ghost rising up from the earth!"

"What does it look like?"

"It's an old man, wrapped in a cloak."

Then Saul heard the voice of an old man.

"Why have you disturbed me?" asked the voice. "Why did you bring me up from the underworld?"

"I'm in trouble!" answered Saul. "The Philistines are ready to attack, and the Lord has turned away from me! He won't answer me anymore! Tell me what to do!"

"What's the use?" asked the voice. "God is doing what he said he would do. He has torn the kingdom away from you and given it to David. He'll let you and your whole army fall into the hands of the Philistines. You and your sons will die in battle, and tomorrow you'll join me in the world of the dead!"

As the voice faded away, Saul fainted.

"Please, my lord," said the woman when Saul opened his eyes. "Take some food. I did as you asked. I put my life in your hands. Now listen to me. Eat so you'll be strong enough to make your way back to camp."

Saul didn't want to eat, but finally his men persuaded him, and he got up, sat on a couch, and ate what the woman prepared. Then he and his men returned to the Israelite camp.

Saul's Last Battle

1 Samuel 31; 1 Chronicles 10; 2 Samuel 1

THE next day a great battle was fought at Mount Gilboa. The Philistines attacked, and the Israelites scattered. The Philistines chased them and killed many, including three of Saul's four sons: Abinadab, Malchisua, and Jonathan.

The battle raged on, with heavy fighting around Saul. Some Philistine archers shot him with their arrows and badly wounded him in the stomach.

"Come here," Saul said to his weapon-bearer. "Draw your sword and kill me, or these heathen will find me and torture me!"

The young man was too frightened to obey, so Saul took his own sword and fell on it. When the weapon-bearer saw that Saul was dead, he fell on his sword and died with his master.

The next day the Philistines came back to the battlefield to strip the corpses. When they found Saul and his sons, they took their armor and weapons and sent them to the temple of their goddess Asherah. Then they nailed the bodies to the wall of the city of Beth-shan.

The people of Jabesh in Gilead heard what the Philistines had done, so the bravest men in the city went and took down the bodies of Saul and his sons. They brought them back to Jabesh and buried them properly. Everyone in Jabesh mourned for them, because Saul had saved Jabesh from blindness many years before.

The people of Ziklag heard what had happened when a messenger came to David.

"Where are you coming from?" David asked.

"I've just escaped from the battle!" he answered.

"What happened? Tell me!"

"Our army has retreated and many of our soldiers have fallen! Saul and Jonathan have been killed!"

"How can you be sure?"

"I was there. I saw Saul wounded and leaning on his spear. The enemy was closing in on him, and he called for me to come and kill him. He said he was dying and he didn't want to fall into the hands of the Philistines, so I killed him. I took the crown from his head and the bracelet from his arm. Look! I've brought them to you, my lord! Your enemy is dead!"

"Who are you?" asked David.

"The son of an Amalekite," the young man answered, "and a soldier in Saul's army."

"How dare you raise your hand against the Lord's anointed king!" cried David, and he ordered a servant to put the man to death.

Then David and his followers mourned and cried for Saul and Jonathan and the other soldiers who had fallen in battle. David wrote a song about the death of Saul and Jonathan, and he sang it as they mourned.

> On the hills of Israel
>   our soldiers lie dead!
> Saul and Jonathan,
>   so strong and brave!
> Jonathan, my friend, my brother,
>   you meant so much to me!
>
> Their armor is useless,
>   their weapons are scattered!
> The warriors are dead,
>   the mighty have fallen!

Stories About David the King

22

Two Kings Mean Trouble

2 Samuel 2

NOW that Saul and Jonathan were dead, David thought it might be the right time for him to become king. But before he did anything, he consulted the Lord.

"Should I go and take over one of the cities of Judah?" he asked.

"Yes," answered the Lord.

"Which one?"

"Hebron."

David took his wives and his men and their families and moved from Ziklag to Hebron, in the middle of Judah. The people of Judah were grateful to him for protecting them from their enemies. They came to Hebron and anointed David as their king.

But about the same time that David became king of Judah, Saul's youngest son, Ishbaal, became king of Israel. Ishbaal was the only one of Saul's four sons to survive the battle of Mount Gilboa. Saul's cousin and commander, Abner, had escaped with him. Abner took Ishbaal across the Jordan to Mahanaim and made him king.

It was a dangerous situation—Saul's weak son king in Israel and David, the leader of his own army, king in Judah.

Many people came to Hebron to support David. They came from all over the land of Israel, but mostly from the territory of Judah. Among them were David's nephews, the sons of his sister Zeruiah. These three brothers, Joab, Abishai, and Asahel, were rough and violent men, but David depended on them. They caused him a lot of trouble.

One day, when David had been king of Judah about two years, he heard that Abner was coming to attack him. He was marching from Mahanaim with an army.

David's men left Hebron with David's nephew Joab in command. They met Abner's men at a pool near the city of Gibeah. One group halted on one side of the pool, and the other halted on the opposite side.

"Let's settle our quarrel with a contest!" Abner suggested to Joab. "Let's have some of the young men from each army come forward to fight in single combat!"

"All right!" agreed Joab.

The men came forward and took their places, twelve on each side. Then each man grabbed his opponent by the head and plunged his sword into his opponent's side. All twenty-four of the contestants fell down together, dead.

Since the contest hadn't settled anything, the two armies fought a battle. Joab lost nineteen men, and Abner lost three hundred and sixty. Then Joab's men chased after Abner's, trying to kill them.

Joab's brother Asahel ran after Abner. Asahel could run as fast as a deer. As he came closer, Abner called back to him, "Is that you, Asahel?"

"Yes!"

"Go chase someone else!"

But Asahel kept running after Abner.

"Stop chasing me!" cried Abner. "You'll force me to kill you! Don't make trouble between me and your brother Joab!"

When Asahel refused to stop, Abner struck him in the stomach with a backward thrust of his spear, and Asahel fell down dead.

Then Joab and Abishai began to chase Abner. They ran after him all day. Just as the sun was setting, they reached a hill.

Abner and his men climbed up to the safety of the hilltop, and then Abner called down, "Joab! Let's stop this fighting! Don't you see where all this killing will lead? Tell your men to stop chasing us. Let's make peace!"

"All right!" said Joab. "It's a good thing you spoke when you did! My men were prepared to chase you all night!"

Joab sounded the trumpet as a signal for his troops to give up the chase. Then he took his men to Bethlehem to bury his brother Asahel. After the funeral they went back to Hebron. Abner and his army returned to Ishbaal at Mahanaim.

23

The Murder of Abner and Ishbaal

2 Samuel 3—4

ISHBAAL was suspicious. He thought Abner wanted to make himself king, and he accused Abner of taking one of Saul's widows as his wife. Someone who wanted to be king often took the wives of the former king.

"How dare you insult me!" answered Abner. "I've always been loyal to Saul and your family! You're treating me like a dirty dog of Judah! Well, Ishabaal, I'm through with you! From now on, I'm going to work for David! I'll make him king over all Israel!"

Now Ishbaal was frightened. He didn't say anything else to Abner.

Abner immediately sent a message to David, offering to help make him king in Israel.

David wanted Abner's help, but he carefully bargained with him. "I'll make an agreement with you on one condition," he answered. "When you come to me, bring Saul's daughter Michal with you!"

If David could get Michal back, he would have a stronger claim to the throne, for he would be the former king's son-in-law. So he also sent a message to Ishbaal. "Give me back Michal!" he said. "She's my wife. I paid for her with a hundred dead Philistines!"

Ishbaal was so afraid, he let Abner take Michal away from her husband and back to David.

Before he went to Hebron, Abner spoke to the chiefs of the twelve tribes of Israel. He said, "You've been wanting David to become your king for a long time. You know the Lord promised to save us from our enemies through him! Well, now's the time to do something about it!"

Then Abner took two of his men and went down to Hebron with Michal. David welcomed him with a feast.

"I'll win all the tribes over to you!" Abner promised. "I've already spoken to the leaders of the tribes, and I'm sure they'll acknowledge you as their king. Then you'll rule over everything you desire!"

After the feast, David sent Abner on his way in peace. When Joab returned from a raid later that day, he found out that Abner had been to see David. He was furious.

"What have you done?" he asked his uncle. "You had Abner in your power and you let him get away! He's not really on your side! He's up to something!"

Then, without telling David, Joab sent some men after Abner. When they brought him back to Hebron, Joab met him and went up to him as if he wanted to talk to him privately. Then he stabbed Abner in the stomach. He murdered Abner to avenge the death of his brother Asahel.

When David heard about the murder, he was horrified. "The Lord knows I'm innocent!" he said. "Even though I'm God's anointed king, I'm powerless to stop these violent sons of Zeruiah! They're too much for me! May the Lord himself punish Joab and his whole family!"

David planned an elaborate funeral for Abner, and he ordered all his people including Joab, to mourn. At the funeral David walked behind Abner's coffin, and when Abner was buried, David cried loudly at the tomb. He even wrote a song about Abner's death.

Everyone heard about David's behavior and believed that he wasn't responsible for the murder. They were pleased with the way he mourned Abner. They were pleased with everything he did.

But when Ishbaal heard the news, his heart sank. He and his followers felt discouraged and frightened. Without Abner's help, how could Ishbaal keep David from taking over Saul's kingdom?

Two of Ishbaal's officers, Baanah and Rechab, decided to act boldly to please David. They went to Ishbaal's house in the middle of the day, while he was resting. They sneaked past the guard and entered the room where Ishbaal was sleeping. They struck and killed him and cut off his head.

Then they sneaked back out of the house and walked all night to Hebron. In the morning they brought Ishbaal's head to David.

"Here's the son of your enemy, Saul, who tried to kill you!" said Banaah.

"Today the Lord has given you revenge on Saul and his family!" said Rechab.

David's answer shocked them. "The man who told me Saul was dead thought he was bringing me good news," said David. "I had him killed. How much worse for you, you criminals! You've murdered an innocent man while he was sleeping in his own bed! You'll be punished for shedding his blood! I'll wipe you off the face of the earth!"

Then David ordered his men to kill Rechab and Baanah and to bury Ishbaal in Abner's tomb at Hebron.

Although he was innocent of the murder of Abner and Ishbaal, with them out of the way, nobody could stop David from becoming king of Israel.

24

David Becomes King of Israel

2 Samuel 5, 21, 23; 1 Chronicles 11—12, 14

THE chiefs of the twelve tribes of Israel were determined to make David their king. They went together to Hebron and said to him, "You led the army of Israel while Saul was still our king. The Lord promised you'd rule over us as the shepherd of God's people."

Then they made a covenant with David and anointed him king of Israel.

People from every part of the land sent supplies for a great coronation feast. Flour and fig cakes, raisin cakes, wine, olive oil, beef and mutton arrived on the backs of donkeys and camels, mules and oxen. For three days the leaders of the tribes celebrated at Hebron with David and his followers.

As soon as he became king of Israel, David decided to move his capital from the territory of Judah. He didn't want his capital to be in the territory of Israel, either. Instead, he chose a city between Judah and the northern tribes—the city of Jerusalem.

Jerusalem had never been captured by the Israelites. This important city in the middle of the hill country was still under the control of the Jebusites. They had been able to defend themselves from their strong fortress on top of Mount Zion.

"Ha! Ha!" laughed the Jebusites when they saw David and his army. "You'll never get into our city! We're so safe, even blind and lame people can keep you out!"

But David knew about a secret passage through the rock on the east side of the city. It was a tunnel the Jebusites used to bring water from outside the city wall.

David showed his men the entrance to the tunnel. "Sneak in through this narrow passage!" he ordered. "The first one to kill a Jebusite will become my commander-in-chief!"

Joab led the attack. He squeezed up through the tunnel under the city wall, and the others followed him, one at a time. David's army emerged right in the middle of Jerusalem!

They defeated the Jebusites and captured the fortress and the city. David appointed Joab as his commander and made Jerusalem his capital. He moved his family from Hebron, strengthened the fortress and the walls, and rebuilt the city. Ever afterward, Jerusalem has been known as the City of David.

When the Philistines heard that David was king of Israel and Jerusalem was his capital, they sent an army to capture him. David and his men went into the fortress while the Philistines camped between Jerusalem and Bethlehem.

"Oh," said David, "How I wish I could have a drink of water from the well by the gate of Bethlehem!"

David's three bravest warriors made their way through the enemy lines and drew some water from the well. But when they brought it back to David, he refused to drink it. Instead, he poured it out onto the ground, as an offering to the Lord.

"This water is too precious to drink!" he said. "These brave men risked their lives to bring it here!"

David's men loved him for that.

Then David asked the Lord, "Should I attack the Philistines? Will you defeat them for me?"

"Go!" said the Lord. "I'll defeat them!"

David led his men against the Philistines, and the Lord gave him the victory. But a little while later the Philistines returned. Again David asked the Lord what to do.

"Don't attack the Philistines directly," answered the Lord. "This time go around and come up from behind, opposite the aspen trees. Attack them when you hear a rustling sound in the treetops, like the sound of marching feet. I'll be marching in front of you to defeat the Philistines!"

David did as God commanded. He waited for the sound of the wind rustling in the treetops, and then he attacked.

During the battle David became so exhausted that a huge Philistine named Dodo was able to capture him. Just as Dodo was about to kill David, Abishai rescued him and killed the Philistine.

David's officers made him promise that he wouldn't go into battle again. "You're the lamp of Israel!" they said. "If you die, our light will go out!"

Then the Lord gave David's army the victory, and they forced the Philistines back into their own territory. The Philistines never controlled the hill country again, and people everywhere were afraid of David and his warriors.

25

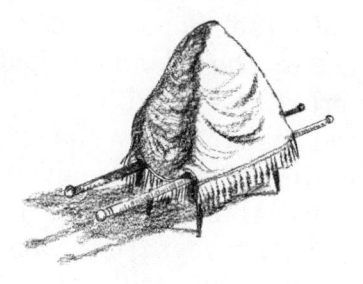

David Brings the Ark to Jerusalem

1 Samuel 6—7; 2 Samuel 6; 1 Chronicles 13, 15—16

AFTER Jerusalem was captured and the Philistines were defeated, David decided it was time to do something about the ark of the covenant. He consulted with his officials and then he announced to the people, "If you approve, and if it's God's will, let's go and get the ark of the Lord our God! We neglected it while Saul was king."

They agreed, and David set off to find the ark.

Twenty years earlier the Philistines had captured the ark. But after the Lord struck them

133

with the plague, they sent the ark to Beth-shemesh, on the border of Israel. Some people at Beth-shemesh had opened up the ark and looked inside. Those people were struck dead, and the others were so frightened that they sent the ark to the city of Kiriath-jearim. There it remained, in the house of a man named Abinadab.

David and the leaders of the twelve tribes went to Kiriath-jearim and found the ark, still in Abinadab's house. They placed it in a special new wagon which they hitched up to two oxen and started to take it back to Jerusalem.

Two of Abinadab's sons, Uzzah and Ahio, led the wagon. Uzzah walked beside it and Ahio walked in front of it.

David and the people with him were so happy about the ark, they danced and sang and played musical instruments. But then something terrible happened.

The oxen suddenly stumbled. Uzzah put out his hand to keep the ark from tipping over, and as he touched it, the Lord struck him dead.

David was upset. He and everyone else felt afraid. "How can I keep the ark of the Lord?" he asked.

He turned off the road and took the ark to the house of a man named Obed-Edom. They left the ark there and then returned immediately to Jerusalem.

A few months later David learned that the Lord was blessing Obed-Edom and his family. David knew that this meant the Lord wasn't angry anymore, so he decided to try again. "This time I'll make sure nothing unholy happens," he said. "Nobody but the Levites must touch the ark. The men of the tribe of Levi are the ones the Lord chose to handle the ark."

David sent for the priests and the Levites and told them to prepare to bring back the ark. "The Lord punished us the first time because you weren't with us!" he said.

This time the priests and the Levites went with David and the others to Kiriath-jearim. The Levites put the ark onto their shoulders with the special carrying poles that fitted through the rings on the top of the ark. They took six steps forward and then stopped while David offered a sacrifice to the Lord.

When the people saw that the Lord was pleased with the offering, they went on their way up to Jerusalem, shouting and singing and dancing with joy.

They entered the city with the sounds of horns and trumpets, the clash of cymbals, and the music of lyres and zithers.

As he entered the city, David was dancing and whirling around in front of the ark. His wife, Michal, looked out of a window and saw him leaping and dancing before the Lord, and she despised him in her heart.

"What a fine day for the king of Israel!" she said that evening, when David came home. "You looked like a fool out there, wearing nothing but a short linen robe and dancing in front of the servant girls!"

"I was dancing to honor the Lord," answered David. "He chose me instead of your father and your family to rule over God's people. If I'm a fool to dance for joy, those servants will honor me for it!"

And to the day of her death, Michal had no children.

For everyone except Michal, it was a day of great happiness.

The Levites placed the ark inside the tabernacle, and David offered sacrifices to the Lord. He blessed the people, and everyone worshiped and feasted together.

Some Levites played musical instruments and

others led singing. Everyone joined together in a great song of thanksgiving to the Lord:

> Sing praises to the Lord;
> Tell about the great things he has done!
>
> Be glad we are his people;
> Let us rejoice, everyone!

26

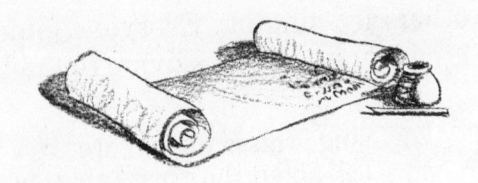

God Blesses David

2 Samuel 3—5, 7—10; 1 Chronicles 14, 17—19, 27

THE Lord blessed David and gave him success. He gave him victory in the land of Israel, against the Philistines, and against other nations.

David fought against the Moabites and the Ammonites in the east, against the Edomites in the south, and against the Arameans in the north. The Lord gave him victory wherever he went.

The Lord also gave David great wealth from his wars, and David dedicated all of it to the

Lord. He stored the gold and silver, bronze and iron in the tabernacle.

All the territory David won in his wars was included in his empire. He ruled from the Egyptian border to the Euphrates River, from the Great Western Sea to the edge of the eastern desert.

David's empire was built at a time when the other nations in that part of the world were weak. Before David's time the Egyptians and the Hittites ruled the area, and after David the Assyrians, the Babylonians, and the Persians conquered it. But for a short period in history there was no great power to challenge Israel's little empire.

David organized his empire and established law and justice for his people. He appointed various officials to run the government, including two wise men, Ahithophel and Hushai, to give him advice.

At about this time people stopped writing on clay tablets with styluses and began writing on papyrus scrolls with ink. Since it was so easy to keep records on scrolls, David appointed scribes to write the history of his reign.

While he was enjoying power and success, David remembered his covenant with Jonathan. One day he said to his officials, "I wonder if any members of Saul's family are still alive. If they are, I want to show them loving-kindness, as I promised my friend Jonathan."

David's officials found a servant of Saul's

family who said that one of Jonathan's sons was still living. David sent for Jonathan's son, and a few days later a crippled man arrived. His name was Meribaal (also called Mephibosheth).

Meribaal had not been able to walk since he was five years old. On the day that his father, Jonathan, had died in battle, Meribaal was picked up by his nurse, who was trying to save him. She was so frightened and in such a hurry, she had dropped him, and he had been lame ever since.

"Meribaal!" said David.

"At your service, my lord," he answered. He looked frightened, because he thought that David might want to kill him. As Saul's only grandson, Meribaal might claim the throne of Israel.

"Don't be afraid," said David. "I want to show loving-kindness for the sake of your father, my friend Jonathan. I'll see that you receive all the property of your grandfather, and I'll make a place for you at my royal table."

"Don't bother with me," said Meribaal. "I'm not important."

David arranged for Meribaal to receive everything that belonged to Saul's family, and he gave him a place at court, along with the royal family.

David's family was large, for he had many wives and children. He had married six women in Hebron and more in Jerusalem. He had taken some of Saul's widows to be his wives, too.

They all lived in a beautiful palace on Mount Zion, the highest hill in Jerusalem. David built the palace with the help of the king of Tyre, who sent him carpenters and stonemasons and cedar logs.

One day David had an idea, so he sent for Nathan the prophet. "Here I am, living in a house of cedar," he said to Nathan, "while the ark of God is in a tent of cloth!"

"Go do whatever you have in mind," answered Nathan. "The Lord is with you."

That night the word of the Lord came to Nathan with a message for David. So Nathan went to the palace the next morning and said to David, "Hear the word of the Lord:

" 'You're not the man to build my house. Ever since I rescued my people from Egypt, I've lived in a tent. I've never asked for a palace, and I don't want one now. Don't you build a house for me!

" 'I took you from the pasture where you were looking after sheep, David, and I made you king. I gave you victory wherever you went. Now I'm going to do more. I'm going to make you famous. I'm going to build a house for you! It will be a royal house, a dynasty! I'll set your family on my throne and your royal house will rule over my people forever!

" 'As for my house—someday I will have a temple. One of your children will build a house for me.' "

After David heard God's message, he went to the tabernacle to worship. He bowed down and prayed, "Lord, who am I, and who are my family, that you have brought me this far? You've done so much for me already, and now you're doing even more!

"How great you are, Lord God! There is none like you! There is no God but you, and no people on earth like your people! All nations have heard of you because of the great things you have done for your people!

"Now, Lord God, I ask you to bless my family

so my royal house will always be pleasing to you!"

God answered David's prayer. He kept his promise and made one of David's sons king after him. This son built a temple as a house for the Lord, and the Lord built a dynasty as a house for David. The people of the house of David, his descendants, ruled over the people of God, for the Lord never rejected David's family as he rejected Saul.

27

David's Sin

2 Samuel 11—12; 1 Chronicles 20

DURING the war against the Ammonites, David stayed in Jerusalem. One afternoon he got up from his nap and walked around on the flat roof of his palace. He saw a woman bathing in her house, and she was so beautiful David sent a messenger to find out who she was.

"That's Bathsheba, the wife of Uriah the Hittite," was the answer.

Uriah was one of David's bravest officers. This spring he was fighting with Joab, attacking the city of the Ammonites.

David sent messengers to bring Bathsheba to the palace, and when she came, he loved her like one of his own wives.

Some time later Bathsheba sent a message to David, telling him that she was expecting a baby. David was afraid, for with Uriah away, everyone would know that David was the father of Bathsheba's baby. He sent a message to Joab to order Uriah back to Jerusalem at once.

When Uriah arrived, David told him to go home and visit his wife. Then everyone would think Uriah was the father of the baby, and David would be out of trouble.

"Go down to your house and visit your wife," said David.

But Uriah didn't go home. He spent the night with the palace guard.

"You've been away a long time," David said to Uriah the next day. "Why don't you go visit your wife?"

"I can't do that!" answered Uriah. "It wouldn't be right while my men are still in battle!"

Then David invited Uriah to eat and drink with him, and he got Uriah drunk. But still Uriah didn't go home. He spent another night at the palace with the soldiers.

The third day David sent Uriah back to the battlefront. He also sent a letter to Joab, saying, "Put Uriah in the front line, where the fighting is the heaviest. Leave him there to be killed."

When Joab received David's letter, he stationed Uriah at a place where the enemy would put up a strong fight. The Ammonites came out of their city and attacked, and some of David's officers were killed. Among them was Uriah the Hittite.

Joab sent a messenger to David with news of the battle. Before he left, Joab said to him, "After you tell the king all about the battle, he may be upset and ask why we went so near the city to fight. If he says anything like that, tell him Uriah the Hittite has been killed, too."

Joab's messenger arrived in Jerusalem and reported to David. When David heard about the battle, he was angry. "Why did you go so near the city wall to fight?" he asked. "Didn't you realize you'd be attacked, that the Ammonites would shoot arrows from the wall?"

"Our enemies were stronger than we were," explained the messenger. "They came out of the city to fight us in the open, but we drove them back to the gate. Then archers shot arrows at us from the wall, and some of your officers were killed. Uriah the Hittite was killed, too."

"Well," said David, "tell Joab not to be upset. You never know who will die in battle. Tell him to keep up the attack until he takes the city."

Bathsheba mourned for her husband, and then David sent for her and she came to his palace to be his wife. Some time later their child was born, and nobody suspected they had done anything wrong.

But Nathan the prophet came to the palace with a message. He told David a story.

"Once upon a time," said Nathan, "there were two men who lived in the same city. One man was rich and the other was poor. The rich man owned many herds of cattle and flocks of sheep, but the poor man had nothing except one little lamb. He took care of the lamb himself, and it grew up in his home with his children. It ate from his dish, drank from his cup, and slept in his lap. The little lamb was like a daughter to him.

"Then one day a traveler came to the rich man's house. The rich man was too stingy to take one of his own animals to feed the guest, so he took the poor man's lamb and served it as a meal for the traveler."

By the end of the story, David was so angry, he burst out, "That man deserves to die! That man was so cruel, he should pay for the lamb four times over!"

"You are that man," said Nathan. "You are the rich man who took the poor man's lamb. Now listen to what the Lord has to say to you:

" 'I anointed you king of Israel and I saved you from Saul. I gave you his wives and his royal house. I would have given you even more if you had asked. But you have disobeyed my commandments! You have taken another man's wife! You have murdered Uriah the Hittite and you have stolen his wife! Because you did this, you and your whole family will suffer. You took Bathsheba in secret, but I'll take your wives and give them to another man in broad daylight! And in every generation someone in your family will die a violent death!"

"I have sinned against the Lord!" cried David. "I deserve to die!"

"The Lord will make you pay for your sin," said Nathan, "but you won't die."

After Nathan left, Bathsheba's child became very ill. David prayed for his son, and he spent the night fasting and lying on the floor in mourning clothes. His officials tried to make him get up and eat, but he refused. He acted like this for seven days, and then the child died.

David's servants were afraid to tell him. "While the child was alive, he wouldn't listen to us," they said to each other. "Who knows what he'll do when he finds out the child is dead?"

David saw them talking together and guessed what they were saying. "Is the boy dead?" he asked.

"He's dead," they answered.

David got up, washed himself, and put on fresh clothes. Then he went and worshiped the Lord. When he came back home, he asked for food and ate heartily.

"What does this mean?" asked his officials. "While the boy was alive you mourned for him. You fasted and cried. But now he's dead, you get up and eat!"

"I mourned while he was alive because I thought the Lord might take pity on me," said David. "I thought he might let the child live. But now the boy's dead, why should I mourn? Can I bring him back again? Someday I'll go where he is, but he'll never come back to me!"

David comforted his wife Bathsheba, and the

following year she had another son. The Lord told Nathan the prophet to tell David to name the boy Jedidiah, which means "beloved of the Lord."

Then David knew that the Lord had forgiven him.

28

The Beginning of David's Family Troubles

2 Samuel 13

DAVID'S oldest son was Amnon, and the next in age was Absalom. The two young men had different mothers, so they were half-brothers.

One day Amnon's cousin Jonadab noticed that Amnon looked sad all the time. "Tell me what's bothering you," he said.

"I'm in love with Absalom's sister Tamar," he answered. "But I can't get near her!"

Jonadab gave Amnon some advice, and Amnon went to bed, pretending to be sick. When his father came to visit, he said, "Please let Tamar come and prepare some cakes for me."

David sent for Tamar, who went and found Amnon lying in his bed. She made him some cakes, but he refused to touch them. He ordered all the servants out of the room and then he said to her, "Bring the cakes over here and serve them to me with your own hands."

As she brought him the cakes, he grabbed her and said, "I love you!"

"Stop it!" she cried, but he wouldn't let go. "Don't act like a beast!" she said, "Don't dishonor me! Don't disgrace yourself! You must ask the king if you can marry me. Please listen. He won't refuse you."

But Amnon ignored Tamar's cries and overpowered her. Afterward, he was filled with deep hatred. He hated her now more than he had loved her before. "Get out of here!" he said.

"Please!" she begged. "Don't send me away! This is worse than what you've already done!"

But Amnon wouldn't listen to her. He called a servant and ordered, "Get rid of this woman! Throw her out and lock the door behind her!"

Tamar ran outside. She took some dirt from the ground and put it on her head as a sign of mourning. Then she tore her long robe and went away, crying out loud.

Absalom found his sister and took her home. "Has Amnon been bothering you?" he asked.

She told him what had happened.

"Be quiet," said Absalom. "I'll take care of him." He told Tamar to stay in his house, and she hid there, lonely and sad.

When David heard what Amnon had done, he was furious, but he didn't punish him.

Absalom hated Amnon so much, he refused to speak to him. But he kept his feelings to himself and watched and waited for a chance to pay Amnon for what he had done to his sister.

One day about two years later, Absalom went to David and said, "I'm having my sheep sheared in a pasture north of here. Would you come and bring the whole family for the feast?"

"Oh, no, my son," answered David. "That would be too much trouble for you."

Absalom asked again, and again David refused. He gave Absalom his blessing and started to say good-bye. Then Absalom asked, "If you won't come, would you let Amnon come?"

David refused again, but Absalom kept asking, so finally David gave permission for all his sons to go to Absalom's sheep-shearing feast.

As Absalom prepared for the feast, he told his servants, "Wait until Amnon is drunk with wine. When I give the order, kill him! Don't worry. I'll take full responsibility. Be bold!"

Absalom's servants watched Amnon carefully during the feast. When he was drunk, Absalom gave the signal and they killed him. The other princes got up and jumped onto their mules and hurried home as fast as they could go.

While they were still on their way, David heard a rumor that Absalom had murdered all his brothers. David tore his clothes and threw himself onto the ground, and so did all his officials.

Amnon's friend Jonadab came in and said, "My lord! Don't believe this rumor! Only Amnon has been killed. All your other sons are still alive."

"What does it mean?" asked David.

Jonadab answered, "Haven't you noticed the expression on Absalom's face these past two years? He hates Amnon because of what he did to his sister."

Just then a watchman reported that a crowd was headed toward the palace.

"Here they come!" cried Jonadab. "Your sons are alive, just as I said!"

The princes came in crying out loud, and David and his officials joined them in mourning.

While they mourned, Absalom escaped to Geshur, where his mother's father was king.

29

Absalom's Rebellion

2 Samuel 14—16

JOAB, David's nephew and commander, was worried. He thought that an angry Absalom in exile might be dangerous. He watched David, and when he noticed that the king had recovered from his grief for Amnon, and was beginning to miss Absalom, he convinced David to let Absalom return.

Joab brought Absalom back from Geshur, but David said, "Let him go to his own house. I don't want to see him."

After two years of staying in Jerusalem and

not seeing his father, Absalom forced Joab to arrange a meeting. He went to the palace and bowed down before David, and David welcomed him with a kiss.

But it was too late. Absalom was already planning to make himself king. He was the king's oldest son, but after what had happened, he knew that David would probably choose another son to become the next king. Before that happened, he decided, he would act.

Absalom was the best-looking man in Israel, with an especially beautiful head of thick hair. He spent the next four years making himself popular with the people, so they would support him when he rebelled.

First he bought a chariot and some horses and hired fifty men to escort him through the city. Then he began to go out early every morning and meet the people as they entered the city gate. He stopped them and asked them about their problems. When he found someone who was taking a dispute to the king, Absalom said, "You have a good case, but the king won't help you. Oh, if only I were in charge! I'd be sure that everyone was treated fairly!"

In this way the handsome prince stole the people's hearts.

When he thought the time was right, Absalom went to his father and asked, "May I have your permission to go to Hebron? When I was in Geshur, I promised the Lord I'd worship him in

Hebron if he'd bring me back to Jerusalem."

"Of course," answered David.

Absalom took Ahithophel, one of David's advisers, and two hundred other people with him to Hebron. Then he sent messengers to every part of the land to tell the people, "When you hear the sound of trumpets, shout, 'Absalom is king in Hebron!'"

He arrived in Hebron and made himself king. Trumpets sounded all over Israel, and many people shouted, "Absalom is king!"

When David heard what was going on, he said, "We must leave Jerusalem at once! Hurry! We must go right away, or we'll be trapped! Absalom will soon be here!"

David left ten of his wives to look after the palace, and he and his supporters walked out of the city.

At the very last house David stopped to watch his palace guard march by. Ittai, a Philistine from Gath, was commander of the six hundred soldiers.

"Why are you coming with me?" David asked Ittai. "Go back to Jerusalem! You're a foreigner—why should you come with me into exile? I don't even know where I'm going. Return home, and may the Lord bless you!"

Ittai answered, "As the Lord lives, wherever you go, I will go, in life or in death!"

"Very well," said David. "March on!"

As David and his supporters walked away

from the city, David noticed the priests and Levites carrying the ark. "Take the ark back to Jerusalem," he told them. "If the Lord is pleased with me, he'll bring me back, and if he isn't—well, let him do what he wants!"

Then David went up to Zadok, a priest who was from a different family than Abiathar. "You can help me," he said. "When you return to Jerusalem, find out what's going on and send me a message. Send your son Ahimaaz and Abiathar's son Jonathan out to the wilderness, where I'll be waiting. I won't do anything until I hear from you."

After Zadok and the others left, David climbed

up the steep side of the Mount of Olives, on the east side of Jerusalem. He was barefoot and his head was covered, as a sign of mourning. He was crying, and all the people with him were crying, too.

At the top of the Mount of Olives David met his friend Hushai. Hushai was dressed in mourning, too.

"You can help me," David said to him. "My other adviser, Ahithophel, has joined Absalom's rebellion. As I've been walking along, I've been praying to the Lord, asking him to ruin the advice that Ahithophel gives to Absalom. Go back to Jerusalem, Hushai. You're too old to come with me, anyway. You can ruin Ahithophel's advice. Tell him you'll serve him, and then report everything to Zadok and Abiathar. They'll send Ahimaaz and Jonathan out to the wilderness with a message for me."

A little way past the Mount of Olives David met a man who was cursing and throwing stones. It was Shimei, a relative of Saul.

"Get out! Get out!" shouted Shimei. "You scoundrel! You man of blood! You murderer! The Lord is punishing you for stealing Saul's throne! He's giving the kingdom to your son Absalom! Your crimes are catching up with you!"

"My lord!" cried Abishai, the brother of Joab. "Why do you let this dog curse you? Just say the word, and I'll go over there and knock his head off!"

"Stay out of this!" David ordered. "It has nothing to do with you. If my own son is trying to kill me, who can wonder at Shimei? Let him be. Perhaps the Lord told him to curse me. Or perhaps the Lord will have pity on me and change these curses to blessings!"

David and his followers walked on, and Shimei walked along the hill beside the road, cursing and throwing stones.

By the time they reached the Jordan River, David and his people were exhausted.

30

Advice for Absalom

2 Samuel 16—18

"LONG live the king! Long live the king!"
An old man was running out of the city gate. "Long live the king!" he shouted again. It was Hushai, David's adviser. He had arrived in Jerusalem just in time to see Absalom enter the city.

"Where's your loyalty to your friend David?" asked Absalom. "Why aren't you with him?"

"I want to support the one chosen by God and the people," answered Hushai.

"Very well," said Absalom. Then he turned to

the man beside him. "Ahithophel," he said, "What's your advice? Now that we're in Jerusalem what should I do next?"

"Go to David's palace," answered Ahithophel. "He left ten wives behind. Take them, and everyone in Israel will acknowledge you as king!"

So Absalom took ten of David's wives in broad daylight, on the roof of the palace where everyone could see.

Then Ahithophel said to Absalom, "I have some more advice. "Let me take some soldiers and go after David tonight. If we catch him now, while he's tired, he won't put up much of a fight. He doesn't have a great army yet. I'll kill him and bring his followers over to you. They'll be like a bride coming to her husband!"

Absalom believed Ahithophel's advice was as good as the word of God. He was ready to follow it, but then he turned to Hushai and said, "Let's hear what you have to say. Should I follow Ahithophel's advice, or do you have a better idea?"

"Ahithophel's advice is no good!" said Hushai. "If you attack David now, you'll be in trouble. David's men are experienced soldiers, and they're so angry now, they'll kill some of your men at the beginning of the battle. Then everyone will say you've been defeated. Your supporters will panic. They'll leave you and go back to David!

"No," continued Hushai, "don't go after David tonight. I have better advice. Take a few days to build up a large army, so you're sure to defeat David's men. Think of the great victory: if David's in the countryside, you'll surprise him like dew falling on the ground! If he's in a walled city, you can drag it down with ropes so no stone will be left! But don't attack now. David's men are as angry and fierce as a wild bear robbed of her cubs!"

Absalom and his supporters didn't realize that the Lord was ruining Ahithophel's good advice and giving bad advice through Hushai.

"I prefer Hushai's advice!" said Absalom, and all his supporters agreed. They didn't go after David that night while he and his men were tired. Instead, they waited to build up their army. But this gave David time to build up his army, too.

Hushai went to the priests, Zadok and Abiathar, and told them what was happening. "Send a message immediately!" he said. "Warn David to cross the Jordan River tonight!"

Ahimaaz and Jonathan, the priests' sons, ran out to the wilderness with the message. "Hurry!" they cried. "Cross the river at once!"

David and his followers crossed the Jordan and escaped into Gilead. When they reached the town of Mahanaim, people came out to meet them, bringing food and supplies.

"You must be hungry and thirsty and tired," they said and gave them wheat and barley, meat, roasted grain, beans and lentils, honey, cheese, sheep and cattle, and blankets and mattresses.

David and his people ate and rested and regained their strength. By the time Absalom and his forces came after them, they had built up a large army.

David divided his troops into three units. As they prepared to march out, he said to the commanders, "I'm going to march with you myself."

"You mustn't come with us," they answered. "If we run away or if half of us are killed, it won't make any difference. But you're worth ten thousand of us! Stay here. You can send help if we need it."

"Whatever you think best," said David, and he stood by the side of the city gate as the troops left. He called after the commanders, "For my sake, deal gently with the young man Absalom!"

David's army met Absalom's army in a dense forest in Gilead. Joab, Abishai, and Ittai led David's forces, and Absalom led his own troops. Absalom went into battle on the back of a mule, the usual custom for kings.

As Absalom was riding through the forest, he passed under the branches of a great oak tree. His beautiful thick hair got caught in the branches, and the mule rode on, leaving him dangling in the middle of the air.

Some of David's soldiers came by and saw Absalom struggling to free himself from the tree. They told Joab, who came and plunged spears into Absalom. Then ten of Joab's men closed in on Absalom and finished him off.

When Absalom was dead, Joab sounded the trumpet to signal the end of the battle. Absalom's army scattered away.

David's men took Absalom's body and threw it into a deep pit. They covered it with a huge pile of stones, burying him like a criminal.

31

News for David

2 Samuel 18—19

AHIMAAZ, the son of Zadok, wanted to tell David about the battle. "Let me run to the king," he asked Joab. "Let me tell him the good news. The Lord has saved him from the power of his enemies."

"No," said Joab. "Today's not the day for you to take news. Another day, perhaps. The king's son is dead."

Joab asked his Ethiopian servant to go and report the news to David. After the man ran off, Ahimaaz said, "Let me run after him!"

"No," said Joab again. "Why do you want to do that? You'll receive no reward for this news."

"Whatever happens, I want to go!"

"Well, then, go!"

Ahimaaz ran off down the road through the wilderness, and he soon passed the Ethiopian.

Meanwhile, David was sitting by the gate of the city, waiting for news of the battle and his son Absalom.

A watchman who was standing on the wall called out, "A man's running toward the city! He's alone!"

"If he's alone, he must have good news," said David.

The runner came closer.

"Look!" called the watchman. "There's another man running alone!"

"This one is also bringing good news!" said David.

"The first one's Ahimaaz!" called the watchman. "I can tell it's him by the way he's running."

"He's a good man," said David. "He'll earn a reward for bringing good news!"

Ahimaaz approached, calling to the king, "All's well!" Then he came up to David, bowed, and said, "Praise the Lord! He has given you victory over the rebels!"

"Is all well with the young man Absalom?" asked David.

"My lord," answered Ahimaaz, "something

was going on when I left, but I don't know what it was."

"Stand over there," said David, and they waited for the Ethiopian.

"Good news, my lord!" announced the Ethiopian as he ran up. "The Lord has given you revenge on all the rebels!"

"Is all well with the young man Absalom?" asked David.

The Ethiopian answered, "May all the king's enemies and all rebels be as that young man is!"

David was so overwhelmed with grief that he

staggered up the steps on the city wall, crying as he went, "O my son! Absalom, my son! My son, Absalom! If only I had died instead of you! O Absalom, my son, my son!"

David stayed in the room above the city gate, mourning his son. When his soldiers returned from the battle, they sneaked quietly into the city.

Joab was so concerned, he went to David and said, "You're acting as if your soldiers mean nothing to you! Those men saved your life! You love those who hate you and hate those who love you! Would you be happy if all of us were dead and Absalom were alive? Now get up and encourage your men! I promise, if you don't, they'll all be gone before the day is over!"

David dried his tears and went down and sat by the city gate. When his men heard where he was, they came and gathered around him.

Just then a messenger arrived with news. People from all over the land of Israel wanted David to come back and be their king. David sent a message to Jerusalem, telling Azdok and Abiathar to ask the leaders of Judah for their support. Then he led his people out of Mahanaim toward home.

People from Judah came to meet David. With them was Shimei, the man who had cursed and thrown rocks at David. He was leading a unit of fighting men from the tribe of Benjamin.

"Please forgive me, my lord," said Shimei.

"Please forgive my disgraceful behavior the day you left Jerusalem. I was wrong, and today I'm the first person from Israel to welcome you back!"

"Don't forgive him!" cried Abishai. "Shimei deserves to die for cursing the Lord's anointed king!"

"This is none of your business, you son of Zeruiah!" said David. "Today isn't the day to put anyone to death!"

Then he said to Shimei, "I promise I won't put you to death!"

Many other people came to David and promised to support him. As he crossed the Jordan, he was escorted by people from Judah and from all the tribes of Israel.

But some people from the northern tribes quarreled with the people from Judah. "Why should the people of Judah be the ones to escort you?" they asked David.

"David is from our tribe!" answered the people from Judah.

"But there are more of us!" said the people from the other tribes. Finally the people from Judah won the argument and they went back to Jerusalem with David.

32

The Census, the Plague, and the Altar

2 Samuel 24; 1 Chronicles 21

ONE day David decided to take a census and count the people, probably to draft more men into his army. "Go to all the tribes," he ordered Joab. "I want you to count the people of Israel, from Dan in the north to Beersheba in the south."

"Why?" asked Joab. "The Lord will multiply the people. Don't do this—it's against the will of God!"

But David insisted, so Joab and the other officers traveled up and down the land of Israel. In nine months and twenty days they counted eight hundred units of able-bodied men in Israel and five hundred in Judah.

But then David began to feel uneasy. "I've sinned!" he prayed to the Lord. "Please forgive me. I've been very foolish!"

The next morning God the prophet brought David a message from the Lord. "Israel must be punished because of this census," he said. "The Lord is giving you the choice of punishment. Which will it be? Three years of famine with no harvest? Three months of attack by your enemies? Or three days of plague with the angel of the Lord killing the people? Give me your answer."

"This is a hard choice!" said David. "But it's better to fall into the hands of the Lord, for his mercy is great, than to fall into the hands of men." So David chose the three days of plague.

The Lord sent disease throughout the land of Israel, killing thousands of people. On the third day David and the leaders of the tribes went to pray to the Lord for mercy. Suddenly they saw the angel of the Lord standing in the sky above Jerusalem. He held a sword in his hand, about to destroy the city.

David and the men with him fell flat on the ground in terror.

"O Lord!" prayed David. "I'm the one who did wrong! It's the shepherd, not the sheep, who has sinned! O Lord, my God! Let your hand fall on me and my family, but spare the people!"

Then Gad the prophet arrived with a message. The Lord wanted David to go to a hill in north Jerusalem and there, on the threshing floor of Araunah the Jebusite, he was to build an altar to the Lord.

David did as Gad said and went where the Lord commanded. He and the leaders of the tribes climbed up to the top of the hill and found a large, smooth rock being used as a threshing floor. Oxen were walking on it, beating out kernels of grain with a threshing board which they dragged behind them.

Araunah and his sons stood watching as David approached. "Why are you visiting me, my lord, oh, king?" asked Araunah.

"I want to buy your threshing floor," answered David. "I'm going to build an altar to the Lord so this plague will stop killing the people."

"Take it," said Araunah, "and do whatever you wish, my lord. Take the oxen and sacrifice them on the rock. Use my threshing boards and the harnesses for firewood. I give it all to you."

"No," said David, "I must pay the full price. I can't give the Lord something which has cost me nothing."

He gave Araunah fifty pieces of silver, and then he built an altar to the Lord. There he sacrificed the oxen and prayed for the end of the plague.

The Lord sent fire from the sky to strike the altar and burn the offering. Then the Lord said to his angel, "It's enough. Withdraw your hand."

The angel put away his sword. Jerusalem was saved.

33

David Prepares a House for the Lord

1 Chronicles 22—26, 28

DAVID wanted to build a house for the Lord, but the Lord built a house for David—a royal dynasty to rule over God's people forever.

Before David died, the Lord chose Bathsheba's son to be the next king. His name was Jedidiah, but he was known as Solomon. He was the one who would build a house for the Lord, a great temple on the rock where David had built the altar to stop the plague.

David wanted to help Solomon. "My son Solomon is still young," he said to himself, "and the house of the Lord must be splendid." He ordered craftsmen to prepare stones for the temple, and he stored materials for the building.

Then he said to Solomon, "My son, I wanted to build a house to honor the Lord, but he wouldn't let me, because I've been a man of war and I've spilled too much blood. The Lord has chosen you to build his house. Your name, Solomon, means 'peace,' and during your reign the Lord will give peace to his people.

"I've prepared the materials for the temple, and you can add more. May the Lord give you the wisdom to follow his teachings! If you obey the Lord's commandments, you'll be successful. Be strong and brave my son, and may the Lord be with you!"

Then David said to the leaders of the tribes, "The Lord is with you, and he'll give you peace. Serve him and build a house for him."

Next David gave special assignments to the priests and the Levites. "The Lord our God has given us peace," he told them. "Now that the ark is here in Jerusalem, you won't have to carry it from place to place. You Levites can help the priests and take care of the equipment in the temple which Solomon will build."

He organized the priests and the Levites into groups of families to take turns working in the temple. Some would be record-keepers, and others would be judges and gatekeepers.

Since David loved music, he paid special attention to the music for worship. "You Levites can sing and play musical instruments in the temple," he told them. He organized them into groups of musicians.

Then David gave his farewell message to the people. "Listen!" he said. "You know how the Lord chose me from all my father's sons to be king. Now he has chosen Solomon from all my sons to be king after me. Solomon will be the one to build a house for the Lord, and the Lord will make his kingdom last forever!

"My people! Study the word of your God, follow his ways, and learn his teachings. Love and serve the Lord with all your heart and all your mind. If you do, he'll let you live in this good land forever!"

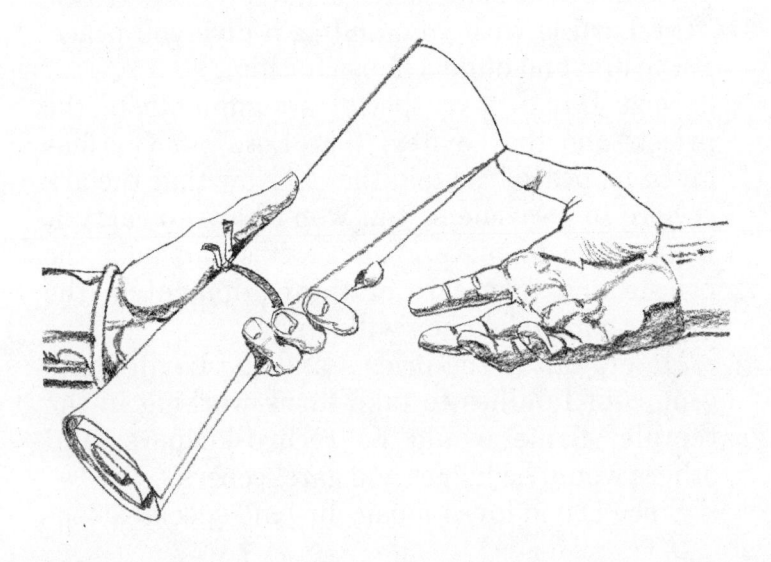

In front of all the people David gave Solomon the plans for the temple and everything in it. "Everything is written according to the Lord's instructions," he said. "Don't let anyone keep you from this important work. Don't be afraid or discouraged. The Lord is with you. He won't leave you. He'll stay with you all the time you build his temple."

Then David said to the people, "This won't be a house for human beings, but a house for the Lord God! I've done my best to help Solomon by preparing materials. I've given silver and gold from my personal treasury, because I delight in the house of my God. Now anyone else who is willing may give an offering to the Lord!"

The people gave joyfully for the temple, and everyone was pleased with the generous offerings. David was so happy, he bowed down and prayed:

"Lord God!" he said. "Yours is the greatness, the power, the glory, the majesty! Everything in heaven and earth is yours! Yours is the kingdom! You are ruler of everything! All wealth and honor come from you! Power and strength are yours to give! Now we offer you thanks and praise your glorious name! These gifts which we give have come from you! We're giving your own gifts back to you.

"O Lord God, keep our hearts and minds turned toward you! Help my son Solomon keep your commandments and obey your teachings!

Help him build the house which I have prepared!"

Then David got up from his knees and said to the people, "Praise the Lord your God!"

They all bowed down and worshiped and praised the Lord.

When David died, he was full of wealth and honor. God's people always remembered and loved David, the man the Lord himself had chosen to be king.

34

A Songbook for God's People

The Book of Psalms

THIS story about God's chosen king begins and ends with singing. Hannah sang a prayer to the Lord in the tabernacle. She sang about God's greatness and how he is the one who makes things happen. God gave Hannah the son she asked for, and he called Hannah's son Samuel to be his prophet. When the people asked for a king, God lifted up Saul. Then he rejected Saul and chose David.

David was beloved by the people and by the Lord. He was a great musician as well as a great

King. He sang when he was happy, when he was sad, and when he wanted to praise the Lord. Some of David's songs and the songs of other people were collected and written down. A hundred and fifty of them are in the Bible, in the book of Psalms.

The book of Psalms is a songbook for God's people. When the temple was built, the psalms were sung during the worship services. God's people met together to praise him, to ask him for help and forgiveness, and to thank him for his blessings.

Sometimes a musician played a simple stringed instrument called a psalter to accompany the psalms.

The words of the psalms are a kind of poetry. Hebrew poetry has rhythm, like English poetry, but no rhyme. Instead of rhyming lines, most Hebrew poems are written in parallel lines. Each group of two or three lines says something slightly different about one idea. In this way, the beauty of Hebrew poetry can be translated into many other languages.

Sometimes the people who wrote the psalms played word games. A few of the psalms are puzzles called acrostics. Each line or verse begins with a different letter of the Hebrew alphabet.

The ancient Israelites loved music and poetry and singing. People of all nations have learned to love the ancient psalms. You can hear them used in worship services all over the world, set to many different kinds of music.

Here are five short psalms, just a sample. You can find more in the Bible and most hymnbooks.

Psalm 121

The Lord Guards His People

Where do God's people turn for help? To the Lord himself. He watches over his people all the time and keeps them safe from every danger.

I will lift up my eyes to the hills—
    Where does my help come from?
My help comes from the Lord,
    Who made heaven and earth.

He will not let your foot be moved—
    He who keeps you will not slumber.
Look, he who keeps Israel
    Will neither slumber nor sleep.

The Lord is your guardian—
    The Lord is your protector on your right hand.
The sun won't strike you by day,
    Nor the moon by night.

The Lord will keep you from all evil—
    He will guard your life.
The Lord will guard your coming and going,
    From this time forth and for evermore!

Psalm 100

Worship the Lord with Gladness

This is a psalm for God's people to sing when they meet together to worship the Lord. Notice how happy they are when they praise him.

Make a joyful noise to the Lord,
    all people of the earth!
Worship the Lord with gladness!
Come before him with a song!

Know that the Lord is God!
It is he that has made us,
    and not we ourselves.
We are his people,
    the sheep of his pasture.

Enter into his gates with thanksgiving,
And into his courts with praise!
Give thanks unto him,
    and bless his name!

For the Lord is good!
His loving-kindness lasts forever,
And his truth endures to all generations!

Psalm 23

The Good Shepherd

This psalm was probably written by David when he was an old man. He compares himself to a sheep and the Lord to a good shepherd. It is one of the most famous and beloved of all the psalms.

The Lord is my shepherd.
I shall not want.

He makes me lie down in green pastures.
He leads me beside the still waters.
He restores my soul!

He leads me in the paths of justice for his name's
 sake.
Even though I walk through the valley of deep
 darkness,
 I will fear no danger,
 For you are with me!
Your rod and your staff, they comfort me!

You prepare a table before me,
 in front of my enemies.
You anoint my head with oil.
My cup runs over!

Surely goodness and mercy will follow me
 all the days of my life,
And I will dwell in the house of the Lord
 forever!

Psalm 127

Everything Depends on God's Blessing

According to this psalm, God's people should trust him completely. He will give his people everything they need and always take care of them.

If the Lord does not build the house,
    the builders work in vain.
If the Lord does not guard the city,
    the watchmen stay awake for nothing.

It's no use rising early and staying up late,
    sweating to make a living.
For God takes care of those he loves
    while they sleep.

* * *

Children are a gift from the Lord.
    He gives them as a reward to his people.
The children of a young man
    are like arrows in the hand of a hero.

Happy is the man who has filled his quiver
    with arrows like that!
His enemies won't shame the man
    with grown sons to defend him!

Psalm 150

Praise the Lord!

The last psalm is a great hymn to the Lord God.

Praise the Lord!

Praise God in his sanctuary;
  Praise him in his mighty heavens!
Praise him for his wonderful deeds;
  Praise him according to his greatness!

Praise him with blasts of the trumpets;
  Praise him with harps and lyres!
Praise him with drums and dancing;
  Praise him with strings and reeds!
Praise him with high, clashing cymbals;
  Praise him with loud clanging cymbals!

Let everything that breathes praise the Lord!

PRAISE THE LORD!

THE WORLD OF SAMUEL, SAUL, AND DAVID

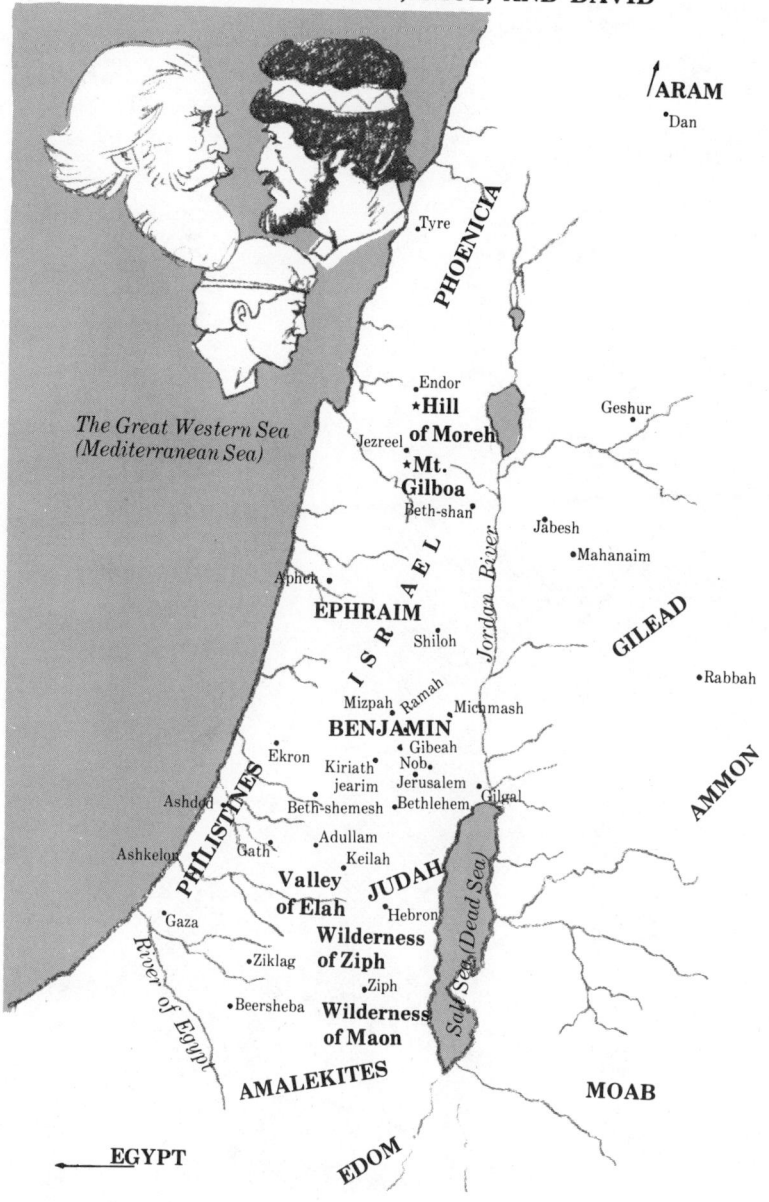

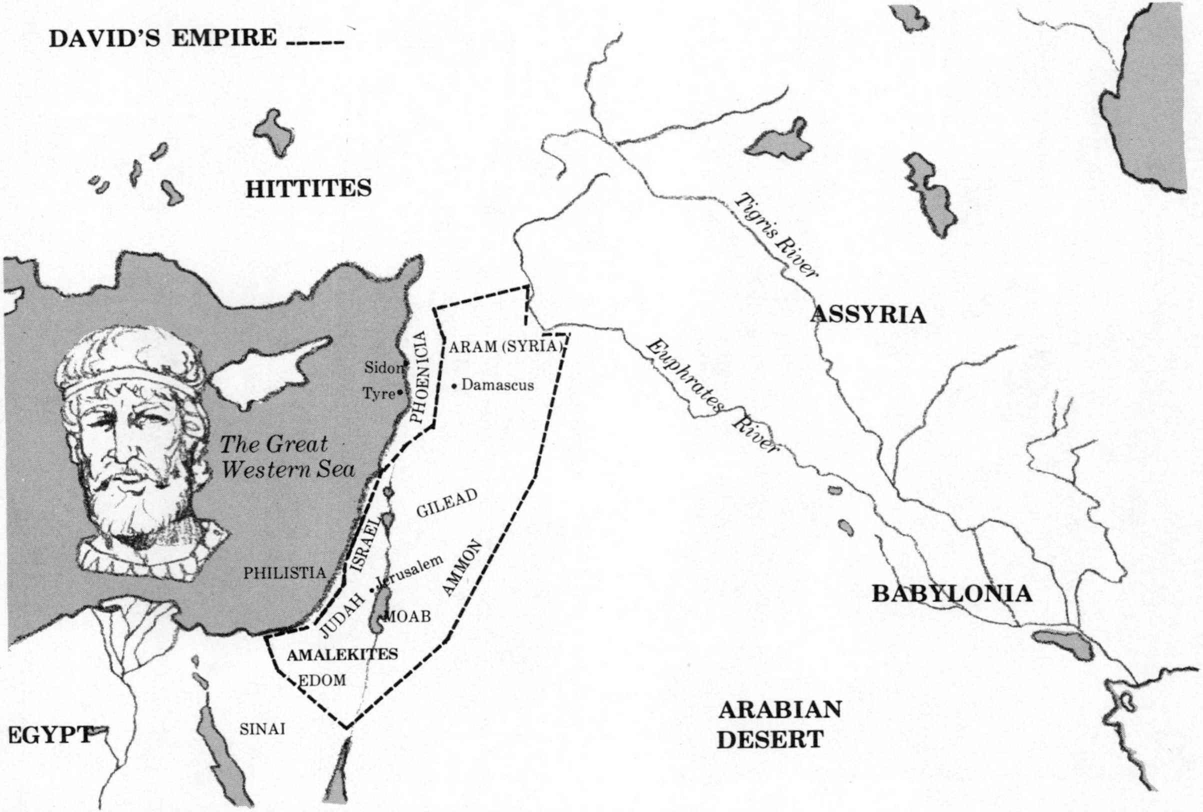
DAVID'S EMPIRE -----
HITTITES
The Great Western Sea
Sidon
Tyre
PHOENICIA
ARAM (SYRIA)
Damascus
GILEAD
ISRAEL
PHILISTIA
Jerusalem
JUDAH
AMMON
MOAB
AMALEKITES
EDOM
SINAI
EGYPT
Tigris River
ASSYRIA
Euphrates River
BABYLONIA
ARABIAN DESERT

Eve Bowers MacMaster graduated from the Pennsylvania State University and George Washington University. She also studied at Harvard University and Eastern Mennonite Seminary. She has taught in the Bible department at Eastern Mennonite College and in the history department at James Madison University, both located in Harrisonburg, Virginia.

Eve visited many of the places mentioned in the Bible while she was serving as a Peace Corps Volunteer in Turkey.

Eve and her husband, Richard, live near Harrisonburg, Virginia, with their children, Sam, Tom, and Sarah.